BUGOTU-ENGLISH/
ENGLISH-BUGOTU
CONCISE DICTIONARY

BUGOTU-ENGLISH/ ENGLISH-BUGOTU CONCISE DICTIONARY

W. G. Ivens

HIPPOCRENE BOOKS
New York

Copyright©1998 Hippocrene Books, Inc.

First Printed, 1940.

For information, address:
HIPPOCRENE BOOKS, INC.
171 Madison Avenue
New York, NY 10016

Cataloging-in-Publication Data available from the Library of Congress

Printed in the United States of America

PREFACE

THE language here represented is spoken on the southern coastal portion of the island called Santa Isabel in the British Solomon Islands. This southern part of the island is known as " Bugotu ". The language was first learned by Bishop J. C. Patteson, of the Melanesian Mission; and a list of his publications in the Bugotu language, which he called " Mahaga ", will be found on p. 525 of S. H. Ray's *Melanesian Island Languages*, Cambridge Press, 1926.

An original MS. edition of this dictionary made considerable use of a card index of the language prepared by the late Mr. Edmond Bourne, of the Melanesian Mission on Santa Isabel. This MS. was unfortunately lost, but its English index was preserved, and many words were recovered thereby.

The material presented below has been gathered in part from Scripture translations in the Bugotu language. These consist of the whole of the New Testament, with considerable portions of the Old Testament, including the Psalms.

Mr. S. H. Ray kindly furnished me with a MS. vocabulary of the Bugotu language, together with an English index, both of which were prepared by the late Rev. Dr. H. Welchman, of the Melanesian Mission on Bugotu. Mr. Bourne's card index, referred to above, had evidently followed Dr. Welchman's MS. fairly closely while adding to his lists. Mr. Ray also allowed me to use a MS. vocabulary of the language which he himself had prepared. His list of words had been drawn in part from Bishop Patteson's material.

I am thus in the happy position of following on all those who have worked on the Bugotu language, and I am honoured to be of their company.

WALTER IVENS.

ABBREVIATIONS

adj., adjective.

adv., adverb.

conj., conjunction.

demonstr., demonstrative.

excl., exclusive, i.e. excluding the person addressed.

exclam., exclamation.

gerund., gerundive.

incl., inclusive, i.e. including the person addressed.

interrog., interrogative.

n., noun.

onomatop., onomatopoetic.

pers., person, personal.

pl., plural.

poss., possessive.

prep., preposition.

pron., pronoun.

sing., singular.

suff., suffix.

vb., verb.

v.i., intransitive verb, i.e. a verb to which the pronouns of the object may not be suffixed.

v.n., verbal noun.

v.p., verbal particle(s).

v.t., transitive verb, i.e. a verb to which the pronouns of the object may be suffixed.

REFERENCES

Arosi, San Cristoval, B.S.I. (unpublished MS. dictionary, compiled by Dr. C. E. Fox).

Ed., Edystone Island (Mandegusu), B.S.I.

Fl., Florida, B.S.I. (unpublished MS. dictionary).

IN., Indonesia.

L., Lau, Mala, B.S.I. "Lau Vocabulary", Ivens. *Memoirs of the Polynesian Society*, vol. ii, 1934.

Lam., Lamalanga, Raga, New Hebrides (unpublished MS. dictionary).

M., Mota, Banks' Islands. *A Mota Dictionary*, Codrington and Palmer, S.P.C.K., 1896.

Mel., Melanesia.

MIL., *Melanesian Island Languages*, S. H. Ray, Cambridge Press, 1926.

R., Roviana, B.S.I. *A Roviana Dictionary*, J. H. L. Waterhouse, Melanesian Mission Press, 1928.

S., Sa'a, Mala, B.S.I. } *A Sa'a and Ulawa Dictionary*, Ivens, Oxford
U., Ulawa, B.S.I.   } Press, 1929.

V., Vaturanga, Guadalcanal, B.S.I. (unpublished MS. dictionary).

NOTES

The order of the letters in this dictionary is as follows :—

a, b, d, e, f, g, h, i, j, ch, k, ngg, l, m, n, ng, gn, o, p, r, s, t, th, u, v.

(*gna*) following a word denotes that the pronouns of possession may be suffixed to the word (noun) in question.

When a verb ends with the suffix *i*, or with a suffix ending in *i*, and (*ni*) appears after it, the meaning is that the verb or compound verb in question takes the transitive suffix *ni* in addition to the first suffix.

Reduplicated forms, where known, are added at the end of the entries in parentheses, if they do not appear elsewhere in the text.

Dr. R. H. Codrington published a grammar of the Bugotu language in his *Melanesian Languages*, Clarendon Press, 1885. A further grammar of the language was published in *Bulletin of the School of Oriental Studies*, London, vol. vii, part i, 1933.

Mr. S. H. Ray, *MIL.*, pp. 527–9, gives the IN. origin of certain Bugotu words.

A DICTIONARY OF
THE LANGUAGE OF BUGOTU

A

a 1, personal article, used with proper names ; used also of particular persons and with relationship terms : *a Soga*, Soga ; *a mama*, father, the Divine Father ; *a Dathe*, the Divine Son ; *a tahigna*, his brother ; *a hanu*, the person, so-and-so, he who ; used with the plural : *iira a taudia*, their wives ; *e vati ara a hanu*, the four persons ; seen also in *ahai*, who ? Sol. Is. *a.*

a 2, exclam., oh ! used in address : *a Moses*, Moses ! *a Jerusalem*, oh, Jerusalem ! V., Fl. *a.*

a 3, suffixed pron. of the object, added to verbs and prep., 3rd pers. sing., him, her, it ; serves as anticipatory object ; added to second member of a compound verb : *e vathovo atua na kavuku*, he sent out a dove ; *vania a Lord*, to the Lord. Fl. *a.*

a 4, verbal noun suffix : *udu*, to walk in file, *uduudua*, companion ; *hiro*, to seek, *hiroa*, a searching, seeking ; *mono*, to dwell, *monoa*, dwelling place, manner of life. S., Fl., *a.*

a 5, (i), adjectival suffix to verbs or nouns ; used also adverbially : *ahoa*, sunny ; *hutua*, big ; *isoa*, little. Fl. *a.*
(ii), passive ending : *hangavia*, opened ; *rotea*, fallen down ; *siria* burnt. Fl. *a.*

a 6, to say, do ; probably the same as *ga* of *gagua*, through the loss of *g* ; see *gua* 1. *ea* Fl. *a.*

a 7, suffix to possessive noun, 1st and 2nd pers. sing. : *ninggua* ; *gamua*. Fl. *a* ; U. *'a.*

a 8, a component part of the gerundival suffix *agna*. *gna* 3 ; *ra* 2. S. *la* ; Fl. *a.*

a 9, pers. pron., 1st pers. pl. incl. ; used compounded with *ti*. Fl. *a.*

aa, to be open, to open, open mouth.

aabara, to crawl along a branch.

aaha v.t., to grate, rub down on a stone, as taro, to sharpen by rubbing. R. *asa.* (*ahaaha*).

aanga v.i., to hurry, hasten ; *adv.* hastily ; precedes vb.
vaaanga v.t., to hasten.

aara, S.E. trade wind. S. *ara.*

aava, a booth, shed ; a lying-in shed.

aba 1, to be wide, spacious ; width.
abaga adj.
abagna v.n., width.
vaaba v.t., to make spacious, enlarge.

aba 2, specific numeral, ten, of turtles ; *sikei na aba*, ten turtles.

abe v.t., to lift up, support ; *abe hadi*, to lift up. Fl. *abe.*
abeagna gerund.

abo v.t., to feed a child with pap.
aboti v.t.

1

abu longa, a southerly wind. *longa*.

ado 1, v.t., to know, know how, can, be wont to. U. *adomai*, to think.

adoagna gerund., knowing, knowledge.

afaafa, to speak or ask humbly ; adv., gently ; follows vb.

agi verbal suffix ; the consonants *g, h, l, m, ng, r, s, v* may be prefixed : *talu, taluagi* ; *havu, havugagi*. S. *a'i*.

agini trans. suffix to vb. ; *taluagini*. S. *a'ini*.

agu, to pick up by handfuls ; a handful. Fl. *ragu*.

aguvi v.t.

aha, to be bitter, sour. S. *ahaa* ; Fl. *ahu*.

ahavagi, to be very angry.

ahai interrog. pron., who ? has indefinite use, whosoever, anyone ; the interrogative *na* may be added : *ahai na*, who ? *na nigna ahai*, whose ? *arahai*. S. *atei*.

ahe, to breathe. Fl. *ahe*.

aheahe, breath. *atheathe*.

aho, sun. S. *sato* ; Fl. *aho*.

vaaho v.t., to dry in the sun.

ahoru, to say ; used at end of sentence, of reported speech : *e ahoru*, saying, said he.

ahu(gna), smoke ; to smoke, of fire ; *ahu i tahi*, sea spray. *ahu i bea*, steam. S. *sasu* ; Fl. *ahu*. (*ahuahu*).

ahuahua adj., smoky.

aia, exclam.

aiani, a natural, an idiot.

achi v.t., to carry under the arm.

achihe onomatop., to sneeze.

ake, exclam.

akeke, eh ! exclam. of pain or fear.

aku onomatop., dog. *auaku*, to bark, of dog. (*auakuku*).

anggai adv., thus, so : *ke anggai*, thus. Fl. *anggai*, this, here.

anggaini v.t. ; *ke anggainia*, thus, do thus to (it).

anggo v.t., to gain, get, of money.

anggume, to be thick, turbid, of water stirred up in a pool.

anggutu, to work in a garden, to work generally ; a garden, work, labour.

anggutuagna gerund.

alevagi(ni), to beckon, wave.

ali v.t., to empty, unload : *ali au*, to remove contents. Fl. *ali*.

aliali nggunggu, to be disturbed in mind, troubled.

alo(gna), shoulder, wing, flipper of turtle.

alu numeral, eight. S. *walu*.

alugna, eighth.

vaalugna, eighth time.

amaama, to beseech.

ana verbal noun suffix with adjectival significance: *matagu, mataguana* ; *siriu, siisiriuana*. V. *ana*.

ane, white ant. Fl. *ane*.

ani 1, demonstr. pron., this, here ; that, there. *ia ani*.

ani 2, v.t., to do, do to, say to ; *hava ati ania na sokara*, how shall we stand ; *ivei katida ania*, what shall we do ? *e ania*, saying, of reported speech ; *ke ania*, he said— *aniagna* gerund.

anga, asthma.

angoango, yellow. M. *angoango*.

angusu, to spit, spit on; spittle. M. *anus*; S. *ngisu*. Fl. *angusu*.

agna gerundival suffix to trans. vb.; the article *na* precedes: *na birehiagna*, to see, seeing, sight; *o tolu na horu i pusiagna*, you struck him three times; *na taviti saniagna*, departure; *u ganiagna*, I ate; *mi manea ke tuguagna na livomu*, and he shall be thy mouthpiece. *a* 8; *gna* 3.

agnu, to shake, of earthquake; an earthquake. *kagnu*. U., Fl. *anu*.

auagnu v.t.

vaagnu v.t.

aoago, to make indistinct sounds, of a child.

aoalo, butterfly, moth.

aoao onomatop.; a bird, crow.

aoaso, to walk.

vaaoaso v.t., to lead by the hand, of child.

apolo, to flap the wings, fly, of bird. (*aoapolo*).

ara, pl. article, used of sets of people; *ara tamamami*, our fathers; *e rua ara dathegna*, his two sons; denotes 'they who': *ara nggounggovu kena havi*, all they who lived. *a* 1, *ra*. Fl. *ara*.

arahai interrog. pron., pl., who? indefinite use, those who. *ahai*.

araara, fish fence of coconut leaves.

arao, a rough basket of plaited coconut leaves for carrying vegetables.

are v.t., to make a feast; *are dokulu*.

areare, a feast, general name.

ari 1, demonstr. pron., that, these; follows noun or pron.: *ia nggeri ari*, that's it there! *ri*.

ari 2, to spread, of vines or roots of trees.

ariri, to shake, tremble, of persons, to shiver as with ague. *aiariri*, to shake, be agitated.

ario, to shout, make a noise. (*aiario*).

aro, to mark with pattern or design; *pohe aroaro*, cloth with patterns.

aroaro, a pattern, design.

vaaroaro v.t., to mark, grave.

aroga, to wink.

aru 1, v.t., to bore, pierce; a pump-drill, gimlet; *aru vula*, to pierce through. (*aruaru*).

aru 2, a tree, casuarina. Fl. *aru*; S. *salu*.

asi, to be wild, of animals, fierce. S. *wasi*; Fl. *asi*.

asikeba, to climb a tree using a rope round the ankles. V. *kalikeba*.

ate(gna), the liver. Fl. *malu ate*.

ati, pronominal verbal particle, 1st pers. pl. incl., we. *a* 9; *ti* 2.

ato, sago palm, sago palm thatch. S. *ato*.

atu 1, to go away, go forth; forth, out, onward; *atuda*, let us be gone! *na taviti atudia*, their going forth. Fl. *atu*.

atu 2, a fish, the bonito.

athaatha, consecutive, in order. Fl. *alaala*.

athaatha vitatha, the beckoning crab.

atheathe, to breathe; breath. *ahe*.

athevotho, to swing the arms, wave, clear away smoke.

atho, cord, rope. Fl. *alo* ; S. *walo*.

athoga adj., stringy.

athoatho, to beckon, signal. Fl. *alo* ; M. *alovag*.

athovi v.t.

au 1, to be out, away ; *au sapa*, to put out to sea ; *moti au atu*, and you departed ; used in compounds : *hagore aua*, to speak out ; *talangi au*, to lead out. Fl. *au*.

aua passive, out.

auau, to put out, of tongue.

au 2, exclam., who can say ? don't know !

au 3, v.t., to take off, remove, as arm ring.

auagna gerund.

vaau v.t., to remove.

auboro, a chief's wife, lady : *ke hadi a auboro*, the lady departs, a division of the day, 11 a.m., the chief's wife leaving the garden work at an earlier hour than her women.

au sumari v.t., to pass through, go beyond. *au* 1.

avini v.t., to carry in the arms.

avusagini v.t., to scatter in the air.

B

The sound of *b* is generally *mb* ; but some Bugotu people sound a pure *b*.

ba disjunctive conj., or ; the vowel of *ba* changes to *e* or *i* in agreement with the first vowel of the following word ; and drops before the locative

i, and also before the initial *i* of the personal pronouns ; *bi . . . bi* denotes ' either . . . or '.

baabala, athwart, across, oblique ; *gai baabala*, a cross. Fl. *vavala*.

baabagnaga, bushes.

baabara, wall, side, of house ; *kongga baabara*, the fastening rod of house door, used for ' lintel '. S. *para*, wall, fence ; Fl. *barobaro*.

babaa, a bird, duck.

babale, booth, shed. V. *babale*.

babao, to be weary.

vababao v.t., to weary.

babi, to be large, of vegetables.

baere v.t., to renew.

bafa, to turn aside.

bage(gna) 1, a bow. Fl. *bage*.

bage(gna) 2, fin of fish, flipper of turtle, wing.

baho, to have sunken cheeks, to be thin.

bahu, to barter food for money, by arrangement between two villages, meeting at a given spot on a path ; a market. Fl. *bahu*. (*baubahu*).

baibalige(gna), armpit.

baka, to be bruised, crushed, broken small.

bakai v.t., to bruise.

bakala, a large paddle. Fl. *bakala*.

bakiha, clam shell ornament worn on chest. R. *bakiha*.

bako(gna), cheek.

bakolo, to fish for garfish from a canoe with a kite.

bali n., thing by which, thing for the purpose of : *bali tatango*, a tool, scrub knife ; *bali puipui*, firewood for the oven ; *na bali kou*, a drink ; *(na) bali vanga*, food, to eat, for eating ; *bali fotalia na ulugna na tinoni*, a thing for breaking men's heads ; *na bali hogoniagna na rongo*, to store treasure in ; *bali hava*, thing for what ? what ? I don't care ! Fl. *male*.

baobalo : *pohe baobalo*, parti-coloured bark cloth.

baorage, to moor a vessel.

baore, to harvest or store almonds ; a store-place for almonds.

barahaha, to be noisy, loud, of noise.

bare v.t., to repair, of house.

baro v.t., to restrain, cause to refrain.

baroagna gerund.

base, to be forked ; *base hangana*, branch roads ; *base rua*, forked, with two members. Fl. *base*.

baebase(gna), member, limb.

baso 1, a twin : *nggari baso*, a twin child. Fl. *baso*.

baso 2, to be compact.

bati, to abstain from, refrain, refuse ; used with *ni* 1. Fl. *bati*.

batu v.t., to lead, precede ; *palu-batu*. U. *qau*, M. *qatu*, head.

batuagna gerund.

bau, fishing net used from tripod on reef.

baubahulu onomatop., a pigeon.

be : *be teo*, or not. *ba*.

bea(gna), water, liquid, juice, Fl. *bea*.

beabeaga adj., watery, tasteless, insipid, without salt ; fresh water.

bebere, to carry in the hand.

beebee v.t., to carry on the hips, of child.

bei, a charm.

beku(gna), hole, grave. Fl. *beku*.

bekukuhagini v.t., to turn the face away from, disregard, slight, despise.

beubekuku, to turn away from.

belama, the frigate bird.   R. *belama*.

beobeleo, to be shaken. *bebeleo*.

beobetho, to partition off, curtain off.

bete, ridge pole. *rapo bete*.

beubethu, to blaze, burn ; a flame.

biabina, large canoe seating fifty men. Fl. *binabina*.

bibi, to be in ear, of grasses or corn.

biibitiana, a sanctuary, tomb and sacrificial altar. *bitiana*. *biti*.

bilaki, to shut, close, of door ; a door : *bilaki savu* v.t., to shut up a person.

bilau, to steal.

bili sisi moro, the anus. *moro*.

bilo v.t., to bore, make hole in plank ; to have holes in. Fl. *bilo*.

bilogna v.n., hole, aperture, breach.

bilomo, to be drowned.

bina, a bird, toucan. Fl. *bina*.

binaboli, to depart, remove ; a stranger, colony of strangers. Ed. *pinausu*, stranger; Fl. *boli*.

binara, a shed, house for storing nuts or yams.

bini v.t., to carry.

biniuki v.t., to undo, to pluck feathers.

binu v.t., to filter, strain, sift ; a filter, strainer.

bio 1, v.t., to extract, pull out, as nail.

bio 2, the chambered nautilus.

biobiroro, to spring up, of plants, to shoot, grow.

birehi v.t., to make, create, begin. *birehiagna* gerund.

biringita, to flood ; a flood.

bisako, shell of canarium almond.

biti, native oven, volcano, sulphur. *bibitiana*. Fl. *biti*.

bithaba(gna), sole of foot.

biu, the areca palm and nut.

biubiru, to shake, wag, of head, to whirl ; a whirlpool. Fl. *birubiru*.

biubiu, a blister.

boabotha(gna), a bruise, scar.

bobo, mountain spur.

bobogno, a tree with seeds like a turtle's back, the seeds themselves.

bobolo, to fear, be in dread of. M. *gogolo*.

boeboe, a platter.

boebone, to act as midwife ; a midwife.

boebote, to conceive, be with child.

bogo(gna), scrotum. Fl. *bogo*.

bohe, to be heavy, weighty ; *gagana bohe*, to think much of, honour. Fl. *bohe*.
bohegna v.n., weight.
boheti v.t., to weigh down.
bohetiagna gerund.

boi, to refuse ; serves as negative particle used with verbs : *ku boi tinoni*, I am not a man ; *na boi na ninggua*, not mine ; *boi nigna*, he doesn't want to ; *ke boigna na nggari duamami*, if the lad is not with us. *bosi*.

boiboila, to refuse, be unwilling.
boitagini v.t., to refuse to do.

boka specific numeral, ten, of *buma* fish.

boke(gna), thigh.

bokihi v.t., to set up on edge, of board or stone, to roll, upset. Fl. *boki*.

boko, widow, widower. R. *naboko*.

boku n., refuse, rubbish ; rubbish heap.

boku nanali, winter.

Bolofaginia, the lord of the dead in Tuhilagi. Fl. *Bolopangina*.

bona, to be distended, full of water, as bag.
bonati v.t., to fill, be full of.
bonatia adj., satisfied.

bongi, night : *ke bongi*, by night, at night. M. *qong*.

boo 1, v.t., to put yams on a stage in *binara*, to leave a thing behind.
booagna gerund.

boo 2, to gather together ; a bundle, company, herd, flock.

boongi, to wedge.

bopa, to dig with a digging stick ; a digging stick.

bora(gna) 1, hole made by animal wallowing, a form.

bora 2, a bird, pigeon. Fl. *bola*.

boro, to be weather-bound, of voyagers. Fl. *boro*.

bosi, negative particle used with verb : *ku bosi adoa*, I don't know ; *e bosi nigna*, he is unwilling ; *bosi imanea na*, is it not he ? *keana bosi ninggua*, but not of, for, me. *boi*.

boto, to be corrupt, decayed, rotten. Fl. *boto*.

botho, pig. Fl. *bolo*.

bouboru, to gush out, flow; a waterfall.

buaburara, to bubble, boil. *ngguanggura*; V. *buroro*.

bubu : *gaugabua bubu*, issue of blood.

buebule, to be foolish, to vex, annoy; a fool, bore, stupid person. Fl. *bule*.

vabuebule v.t., to annoy, vex, trouble; worry.

bugae, to rise up, start, lift up.

bugoro, to be quiet, silent, meek, gentle. (*buobugoro*).

bugorogna gerund.

vabugoro v.t., to silence.

bule, perhaps; *na bule, ka na bule*, perhaps; these two latter forms occur at beginning of sentence, and may be followed by a gerundive. Fl. *bule*.

buibuli i nae, ankle.

bulou, to grow, increase rapidly in size.

bulungoungou(gna), beard.

buma, a fish, sardine. Fl. *buma*.

buriti(gna), rear, back : *buritigna vathe*. S. *puri*; Fl. *buriti*.

busi, sago palm thatch.

buta, to open, of eye, to stare, bulge, of eyes : *ke hahi na buta*, I can't see properly.

butangi v.t., to open, of eye, stare at, behold.

vabutagna gerund., causing to see.

buturu, to be deserted, of place.

buubulu : *pohe buubulu*, bark cloth partly dyed.

buuburu, grass.

buubutu, to stamp the foot in dancing, tread hard.

butuli v.t., to trample, kick.

butuliagna gerund.

butungagi v.t., to withstand.

buugulu, a grove of canarium almond trees or breadfruit : *na buugulu i ngali*, a grove of canarium almond trees.

D

The *d* is generally sounded as *nd* ; but it is sometimes sounded as pure *d*.

da 1, verbal particle, denotes future, has imperative and conditional uses as well ; when the sense is future, *da* is used with the v.p. *ke, kena* ; *kuda, koda, keda, kedana, kenada* ; *kuda taviti* I shall go ; *da anggai hina*, that is what you must do ; *da sokara, da silada*, arise, shine ! *koro da sopou*, let them sit ; *ba da gagua*, or to say ; *da mono e lima*, if there be five.

da 2, suffixed pron. of possession, 1st pers. pl. incl., our : *atuda*, let us be off; *raraida*, let us awake ; *limada*, our hands.

dadaga adj., dry, of land, without water ; dryness.

dadaha, to wash the face.

dadali, to be smooth, level, even, polished. S. *madali*.

vadadali v.t., to smooth, etc.

dala 1, flat round ornament of clam shell overlaid with filagree work of turtle shell. R. *dala*.

dala 2, to fish for garfish with a kite. Fl. *dala*.

dani, morning, daylight : *dani hage*, till morning, all night ;

talu dani hagea, to put a thing away till morning. Fl. *dani*; S. *dängi*.

dao, to go bonito fishing.

dara, mist, fog; to be misty, foggy.

dathe(gna), child, son, daughter: *dathe vaivine*, daughter; *dathe i mane*, son; *dathe i botho*, young pig. S. *kale*; Fl. *dale*.

daudamu, rashly, hastily; follows verb.

daudau, to fish.

davi, pearl shell, breast ornament of pearl shell. Fl. *davi*.

deedee, to be raw, uncooked, unripe.

deedenge, ear ring.

dere v.t., to cut off, lop, of branch. F. *dere*.

deri, a gourd.

dia suffixed pron. of possession, 3rd pers. pl., their: *limadia*, their hands.

didingi v.t.: *didingi nae*, to walk with mincing gait.

dika, to be bad, evil, wrong; evil, badness: *dika hehe*, grief, to grieve, be sad, to bear ill will; *na dika*, wrong, evil. Fl. *dika*.

diadikala v.t., to harm, damage.

diadikalagagna, to fall, of the countenance.

dikata-(gna), anger: *ke dikatagna*, he is angry.

vadikalagini v.t., to spoil, corrupt.

vadikalagna v.n., injury.

veidikahaginigi, to hurt one another.

veidikahehegi, to be at enmity with one another.

doa, to be blind. Fl. *doa*.

doadoka, to look about.

dodo, firefly.

dodolu, to be round in shape.

doka: *puni doka*, pitch darkness. V. *doko*.

dokulu, a chief's feast: *are dokulu*.

domu: *pohe domu*, dark coloured bark cloth.

domurihi v.t., to wreck, of vessel.

vadomurihi v.t., to wreck.

vadomurihiagna gerund.

donga, the wooden image hung at prow of war canoe.

doodoro, to gaze, behold, watch: *doodoro leeleve*, to look askance, envy, be jealous.

doodorogna v.n., gazing.

dorovi v.t., to watch, look at: *dorovi sousopu*, to gaze steadily at.

doroviagna gerund.

veidorovigi, to gaze at one another.

dorokovili, a lizard.

dotho, a free gift, love (late); to be generous, tame, of animal or bird. Fl. *dolo*.

dothovi v.t., to make a free gift to, to love.

dothoviagna gerund.

vadotho v.t., to tame.

veidothovigi, to love one another; mutual love.

dou, corner.

doudou i nae, heel.

dua(gna), companion, fellow; with, of accompaniment: *duagna*, with him, accompanying him; *a duamu*, your companion; *vuha dua i nggaringgu*, from my youth. *faidu*: *haidu*.

duaduala, to increase in numbers.

vaduaduala v.t., to cause to increase.

dudu, to stamp, with the foot.

duduli v.t., to stamp down.

duduli, a bass drum of bamboo; to drum.

duee, to cook vegetable food in a bamboo; the bamboo used for the purpose, a wooden dish, bottle (late). Fl. *duke*.

duili, to challenge to fight; a champion.

duki, a yellow, vinegar ant, with painful bite. Fl. *duki*.

duku, a sack.

duru, onomatop., a bird, owl. Fl. *duru*; V. *kuru*.

duulagi, to spread, of news or fame. Fl. *duulagi*.

duulali, to sound, resound; a sound.

E

e verbal particle, without tense significance; used of 3rd pers. sing. only; has the meaning 'it is', 'there is'; used with the numerals from 'two' to 'ten': *e tutuni*, it is true, verily; *e a e ania, e gagua, e ahoru*, saying, of reported speech; used with *na* 4. to denote 3rd pers. pl.: *ena ahoru*, they said; coalesces with *ma*, and, *ba*, or: *me vuevugei*, and (it was) next morning; *be teo*, or not; used with *minggoi, gua*, lest, *nggi*, illative. S., Fl. *e*.

ea, saying, done, did thus; *ivei ea*, how do? how is it? *e hava ea*, what (is done)? *a* 6; *e*.

eeni demonstr. pron., this, here. *ni* 5.

eeri adv., here. *ri*.

ehu, sugar cane. S. *oohu*.

ei v.t., to do, do to, say: *ei vathe*, to build houses; *ei tidatho*, to practise magic; *ei fata*, doings, acts. In use as a prep. with the pronoun of the object suffixed in agreement with a pronoun following: *eigna na hava*, why? *einggu, einggu inau*, for me, on my behalf; *eida igita*, for us. The article *na* may precede: *na eidia na botho*, concerning the pigs. Other uses in the texts are probably a following of the Mota *ape*.

eiagna gerund., the doing of it, all about it.

enggo, to lie down, sleep, dwell, to be. S. *eno*.

ele, shark.

eli, to be winding, crooked, of path, to err.

elo(gna), a leaf. (*eloelo*).

ena pronominal verbal particle; used of 3rd pers. pl. *e. kena*.

eni adv., here. *ni* 5.

e ngiha, how many, as many. *e*.

eoeto, to wag the head, to rock, of ship.

etoeto v.t., to winnow.

eri demonstr. pronoun, this, that; follows noun or pron. *ri*.

ero, to turn the face away, look away, turn round. (*eoero*).

erohagini v.t., to turn away from.

eta, up, east : *i eta*, up, east ; *i etagna*, to the east of. The *ita* which the Spanish discoverers of the Solomon Islands added to the native name *Mala*, of the island lying east of Santa Isabel, is probably for *eta*.

etieti, areca nut.

eu, to be about to, begin to, to have just done ; precedes a verb ; *eu turugu*, to begin ; *kena eu mono*, they first dwelt.

F

fa causative prefix to verbs : *faeiei* ; *fasiisiri. va* 2.

faefaje, carelessly, heedless ; follows vb. : *rongovi faefaje*, to fail to pay attention when spoken to.

faeiei v.t., to annoy, displease, offend. *ei*.

fafarangagi v.t., to curse.

fafate, the shell of canarium almond.

fafi v.t., to tie between two sticks, clip.

fafiagna gerund.

fafota, thread.

fagila, to watch, perceive, mark, heed : *ko sagoi faifagila*, do not pick and choose.

fahaihali v.t., to provoke. *fa*.

fai, verbal prefix denoting reciprocity : *faidu*. S. *hai*.

faidu, to be on friendly terms with one another. *du* ; *haidu*.

fainoino, to be low, of voice, to speak humbly. *fa*.

fakane, to divine, using a broken coconut shell, to run the eye along a thing to see if it is straight. *fa. kaekane*.

fakedo : *taulagi fakedo*, to live together again, of man and wife, after having separated.

famaemane v.t., to exalt oneself, vaunting. *fa*.

faoioni v.t., to obey. *fa*. *faioionigna* gerund.

fapilau, temporarily, a little while : *mono fapilau*, to sojourn.

faralegai, hamlet.

fari, to share ; precedes vb. and denotes ' together ', ' mutual ' : *fari hagore*, an agreement ; *fari tango*, to work together ; *fari gani*, to share food. M. *var. veifaifarigi*, to share, distribute among one another.

farifi, to huddle up to, keep close to.

fasiisiri, to win, conquer, overcome, be bold : *kati fasiisiri vanira*, we overcame them. *fasiisiriagna* gerund.

fata 1, thing : *na fata i tomaga*, inheritance ; *hai fata*, a thing of no consequence ; *na nago i fata*, treasure.

fata 2, tier : *hage fata*, to go in pairs. S. *ha'a*. *faafata*, layer, kind, rank. *faafataga* adj., in tiers.

fate, to judge ; a judge : *fate haliu*, to acquit ; *fate kathe*, to condemn ; used with *ni* 1 : *keda niu fate katheugna na koakoa*, I shall be judged for my sins. *fateagna* gerund.

fatoli v.t., to break up, of clods.

fauchuu, to be downcast, of countenance, to pout, sulk (*faufauchuu*).

feferi, a numeral, hundred thousand, used of canarium almonds : *na feferi*.

fei, fish.

feilange v.t., to shave by depilation.

feo v.t., to break into a house.

fero, spider's web used as bait with fishing kite, *dala*, for garfish.

figu v.t., to rend, tear in pieces.

fiifidi, to be thin, lean.

fike v.t., to break firewood by hitting it on the ground or on a stone.

file, a bundle.

filehi v.t., to make into a bundle.

fiofigno(gna), point of fish-hook, knife, etc. ; to be pointed, sharp.

firi v.t., to bind, lap with string : *firi ulu, fiifiri ulu*, a head fillet ; *fiifiri*, to twine. M. *vir*.

fiifiriagna gerund.

firikoi, to wrest.

fofohu, to tattoo.

foko(gna), foundation, bottom row of stones in wall : *foko hadi*, to lay foundation, to pile up (*fofoko*).

fota v.t., to break, smash up ; to be broken. S. *pota*.

fotali v.t. (*foafotali*).

foufotu, snake.

fuafuagna, beauty, beautiful.

fufula(gna), bung, plug, cover, cork ; to stop up, stuff up.

furoma, rotten, of trees, hollow.

futu, to gush out, bubble up, boil, of water; a spring. S. *huuhuu*.

fuufutu, to well up, of water, increase in size, of children or animals, to sweat with heat.

G

The sound of *g* in Bugotu is what Codrington calls the 'Melanesian *g*', not a hard *g*.

ga 1, possessive noun, used of things to eat and drink, also with words denoting 'friend' or 'enemy'. The pronouns of possession are suffixed, and the article *na* may precede : *na gagna na bea*, his water to drink ; *ro gadia na thevu i oka*, their enemies. Fl. *ga*.

ga 2, adjectival suffix, added to nouns : *beabeaga*, watery ; *faafataga*, in layers ; serves as noun suffix : *hadiga*, height. Fl. *ga*.

gaagatha tangi, to bewail, be sorrowful. *tangi*.

gaba 1, to stretch, stretch out, of hand ; used with *ni* 1.

gaba(gna), palm branch, a crook. S. *'apa* ; Fl. *gaba*.

gada, to oscillate, move.

gaea adj., furtive, deceitful ; *boi gaea na matagna*, innocent, open countenance.

gaegape, to mount by steps, to climb.

gaegarere, to rustle in the wind, shake.

gaga, fishing line.

gagaa, to draw a bow.

gagala, a fuel heap : *gagala joto*, a beacon fire.

gagi verbal suffix : *havu, havugagi*.

gagiri hagetha, door post.

gagua, to say, do ; *ivei keda gagua,* what shall he do ? Used of reported speech. Fl. *gagua.*

gahe, to boast. Fl. *gahe.*

gaegahe, to boast, to be vain, to be a hypocrite.

gahira, rock, stone.

gaho, rafter. M. *gaso.*

gaogaho v.t., to set up a booth with rafters.

gaogahogna gerund.

gai(gna), tree, shaft of spear. Fl. *gai.*

gaigali, to move to and fro, shake, rock.

gailiga 1, divisions in gardens marking different ownerships ; 2, a length of house thatch. Fl. *gailiga.*

gajika, to cough ; a cough. *kajiga.*

gala, a fishing net.

galalu v.t., to carry on the shoulder.

galaluagna, gerund.

galao, to sound, of voice, trumpet, to lift up the voice ; a loud noise, shouting.

vagalao v.t., to lift up, of voice.

galofa, to have an unpleasant smell.

galume, to decay.

gama, the morning star. Fl. *gama.*

gami, we, us (excl.). Fl. *gami.*

gamu, you.

gana, to think. Fl. *gana.*

gaagana v.t., to think, think of : *gaagana tautu*, to be determined, decided, in mind ; *gaagana pedo*, to make a mistake, be mistaken ; *gaagana ruarua*, to be undecided, doubt ; *talu gaagana*, to keep in mind.

gaagana(gna), thought.

gani 1, to eat up, consume. Fl. *gani* ; L. *ani.*

ganiagna gerund.: *u ganiagna,* I ate.

veigaiganigi, to eat up one another.

gani 2, to hold.

gano(gna) 1, fruit ; 2, to be full grown, ripe : *mane gano*, an adult. V. *hanoa.*

gagna gerundival ending : *diadikalagagna ; toetokelagagna.*

gaogado v.t., to imagine, meditate upon.

gaogaro(gna), the ribs. S. *karokaro.*

gaogarohu, to roar, of beast.

gaohi v.t., to draw, bend, of bow.

gagao, to draw, bend, of bow, to draw a paddle towards the body in paddling.

gaonggai, so ; follows *vagagna*, as.

gaota, to be convalescent, recovered from illness. Fl. *gaota.*

vagaota v.t., to restore to health.

garani v.t., to be near, near to. S. *kara'ini.*

garaniagna gerund.

garige, near ; *garigeigna*, near to, of place ; followed by *i* 3 : *garige i vahu*, the temples.

garo, a lizard ; lives on coconut palm.

gasi v.t., to make a mark with charcoal.

gatha 1, to kindle, burn, glow, of fire ; flame. Fl. *gala.*

vagatha v.t., to fit two ends together, kindle fire with two fire-sticks, to light a pipe.

gathaga, to go up ; up, south-east. S. *'ala'a* ; Loh, Torres Is., *garaga*.

gathapaku, to endure, be patient, long-suffering. *paupaku*.

gathati v.t., to sting, bite. Fl. *gala* ; S. *'ala*. (*gaagathati*).

gatha umi, to jump over. Fl. *gala omi*.

gathautu, firewood, firebrand. *gatha* 1.

gathavahu v.t., to lift the forehead, be proud. *vahu*.

gathi, few, somewhat, small ; precedes vb. : *gathi ngiha*, very few, too few ; *u gathi havi mua*, I am fairly well. S. *kele*.

gatho, cord, rope, line. Fl. *galo* ; S. *walo*.

  gathomi v.t., to roll string on the thigh, wind, twist, turn.

gathotho, to twist, turn round and round. *gatho*. M. *galolo*.

gau, bamboo, sliver of bamboo used as knife, steel knife (late). Fl. *gau*.

gaugabu, a plant, coleus. Fl. *gabu*, blood.

gaugabua(gna), blood. Fl. *gabu* ; S. *'apu*.

gaugauri, to be safe and sound.

gaula, to be cold, damp ; n., cold : *na bea gaula*, cold water ; *ke gaula na hehegna*, he is famished.

  vagaula v.t., to cool, make cold. *vagaulagna* gerund.

gaura v.t., to patch, mend ; a patch.

gauratu, a bamboo. *gau*.

gehe(gna), alone, self, of own accord : *imanea gehegna*, he himself ; *manea ke vathehe*

gehegna, he killed himself. *hege*. M. *gese*.

geli v.t., to dig. M. *gil*. (*gegeli*).

geigesi v.t., to provoke, urge, stir up.

  veigeigesigi, to encourage one another.

geu, to thrust one's hand into a bag. Fl. *nggeu*. (*gegeu*).

  geuhi v.t., to dip into something, of hand or article.

  geuhiagna gerund.

gi trans. suffix to vb. : *jathe, jathegi* ; used with reciprocal prefix *vei* : *veihaohagoregi*.

giagila 1, to cry out, shout.

giagila 2, to reach ; denotes ' until ' ; used with the locative *i* and a verb : *kiti giagilai taviti sania*, till we left him ; *nggi e giagilai*, until.

giagina, to be shy, timid.

gibei, scent.

giigidi, to be in agony, to suffer ; agony.

gigiri, to grin, show the teeth, of a dog ; a saw (modern) ; *gigiri kei*, to gnash the teeth. Fl. *giri*.

giju, a cape, of land.

gini trans. suffix to vb. : *vahothagini*.

gireigna, scab.

giri 1, to be ripe and hard, of areca nut.

giri 2, v.t., to bind.

gita, we (incl.). Fl. *gita* ; U. *ki'a*.

githatha v.t., to know, be aware of, recognize. M. *gilala*. *githathagna* gerund.

giugiu v.t., to prop up, stay. *giugiuagna* gerund.

go 1, suffixed pron., 2nd pers. sing., thee, of object.

go 2, conj., lest; used only with v.p. *e, ena* following; *minggoi* may be added.

godo, to fast till the fulfilment of a pledge or vow; a vow. Fl. *godo*.

goee, to wither, be withered; dried up.

gofe, spider.

gogo, to escape, flee; used with *ni* 1. Fl. *gogo*.

gogohagini v.t., to flee from, escape.

gogoto(gna), thigh.

gogovi, a tidal wave.

gohi adv., already; follows vb.; used to denote definite past time.

goho, to commit adultery.

goi adv., again (of repetition), also, at all, with negative v.p.; used to denote 'change'; precedes vb. Fl. *goi*.

goigori v.t., to shave the head. M. *gor*.

goro, to turn: *goro kilili*, to turn round. Fl. *goro*; R. *gore*.

goromagi v.t., to overflow, overwhelm, of flood; *goromagi mai*, to assemble; *goromagi vano*, to disperse.

gotohi, to stretch of arms or legs, to stretch the body. Fl. *goto*.

gotohiagna gerund.

vagoto v.t., to stretch, of line.

gothahi v.t., to rub or scrape clean or smooth. (*goagothahi*).

gogotha, to rub, plane.

gothapa, to be wide or deep, large, of nuts. Fl. *volapa*.

gua 1, adv., also, more, still, again (of addition), yet, with negative v.p.; follows vb. Fl. *gua*.

gua 2, used of reported speech: *ke hagore gua*, he said thus—. *gagua*. R. *gua*.

gua 3, lest; may be followed by v.p. *e*: *gua oro thehe*, lest you die; *gua e fota*, lest it break.

guagua onomatop., white cockatoo.

guaguna, to be disturbed, be in turmoil. Fl. *ngguna*.

guagunali v.t., to disturb, upset, confuse.

gualuve, betel pepper. V. *kua*.

gua ri adv., perhaps, haply; follows vb. Fl. *gua ri*.

guba(gna), smell; to smell something.

gubaga v.n., a pleasant smell.

vagubaga v.t., to season.

gue, rattan cane. S. *'ue*.

guema, a fishing-rod: *lopo i guema*, a measure, from fingertip to elbow-joint.

gugu(gna), hoof, claw. Fl. *gugu*.

guugugu(gna), finger- or toenail.

gugula, a tree, iron wood, used for side posts of house. Fl. *gugula*; U. *'u'ula*.

guguvu, to be hot; heat: *pono guguvu*, to be in mental distress. Fl. *guvuguvu*.

guigui, to whistle. Fl. *gui*.

guiguli(gna), skin, bark. Fl. *guli*.

guliti v.t., to flay, skin.

guihage, to paddle.

gujuri v.t., to wipe. *ujuri*. Fl. *guduri*.

gulu, to be heavy, of rain: *uha gulu*, to rain in torrents. Fl. *nggulu*.

guri, wind. Fl. *guri*.

    guiguri, to blow, of wind.

    guigurihi v.t., to blow upon.

    guigurigna gerund.

guu, to cry out ; a cry. Fl. *guu*.

    guuvi v.t., to hail, cry to a person.

gutu, a louse. Fl. *gutu*.

H

haa 1, to breathe out.

haa 2, a landing place.

habira, to climb a tree, using hands and feet.

hadi, to rise, go up, used of moon and stars ; adv., up, high ; *ke hadi na hehenggu,* I am displeased ; *hujuu hadi,* to raise the price of a thing. (*haihadi*).

hadi(nga), going up, ascent.

    hadiga v.n., height.

    vahadi v.t., to set up.

hagalu, reef, sea. R. *sagaru* ; Fl. *hagalu*.

hagata(gna), a company, armed band.

hage, to enter, to leak, of canoe : *talu hage.* M. *sage.* (*haehage*).

    hageagna gerund.

    hageli v.t., to put on board, get on board canoe.

    hageviagna gerund.

    vahage v.t., to put on, of arm ring, clothes.

hagetha(gna), doorway : *boibongi hagetha,* side posts of door ; *hagetha i vathe,* front of house. *hage.*

hagini trans. suffix to vb. : *gogohagini* ; *veidikahaginigi.* U. *ha'ini.*

hagore, to speak, say : *hagore tugu,* to answer ; *fari hagore,* to agree in conversation, make an agreement ; *sakai hagore,* covenant ; *sakai hagoregi,* to make a covenant ; *hathe hagore,* counsel ; *talu hagore,* to promise.

    hagore(gna), word, language.

    hagoreagna gerund. (*haohagoreagna*).

    farihaohagoregi, to talk with one another.

    veihaohagoregi, to converse, discuss.

hahaga, to poison fish with *vutu,* etc., to die of a plague, used of numbers.

hahangga, to be unfilled, of bunches of bananas : *hahangga vanga,* to be greedy.

hahali adv., always, much ; follows vb.

hahagna, to be diligent, persevere.

hahi, to err, be mistaken : *hahi ninggua,* I was in the wrong, I could not make it out ; *iju hahi,* countless. Fl. *hahi.*

    hahilagini v.t., to forget, be in ignorance of.

    vahahi v.t., to cause to err.

hai 1, indefinite pronoun, anyone : *me ke teo sa hai,* and there was no one. *ahai.*

hai 2, verbal prefix : *haidu.* S. *hai.*

hai 3, in vain, by chance ; precedes noun or vb. : *hai hagore,* vain words ; *hai tinoni,* a stranger, person of no consequence ; *hai pada* v.t., to happen by chance ; *hai lasa,* to be negligent, do casually, rashly ; *hagore hai lasa,* to blaspheme ; *hai pagana*, to lack, be of none effect.

haidu v.t., to assemble, meet together, meet ; together : *soni haidu*, to assemble ; *vathe i haidu*, a meeting-house ; *kena vanga haidura*, they ate together. *du. faidu.* Fl. *haidu.*

haiduvi v.t., to surround a person.

haiduviagna gerund.

hangga, to lack, be short of ; want, adv., hardly, nearly, almost, to begin to, about to ; precedes vb. : *hangga teo*, hardly, scarcely ; *ku hangga nere*, I want to sleep. Fl. *hangga.*

hainggoinggoi(ni) v.t., to waste, do for naught.

hanggomi v.t., to take aside.

hanggu, to be steep.

hangguli v.t., to climb up a steep place.

haliu, to miss the mark, fail to meet, escape ; adv., perverse, contrary ; follows vb. : *thovo haliu*, to leap out of the way, pass by a place ; *liu.* Fl. *haliu.*

haihaliu adv. : *teo haihaliu sikei*, never a one.

haliungi v.t., to escape : *taviti haliungi*, to travel right through.

haliugna v.n., missing, escaping.

tatahaliu, all along, continuance. *tata.*

veihaliuvigi, to pass one another.

halu, to go : *halu atu*, gone by, past ; *halu tavoga*, to be perverse, contrary ; *halu tabo*, to be disorderly, do mischief ; *halu hadi*, exalted. (*hauhalu*).

haluvi v.t., to follow.

haluviagna gerund.

haludotha, to disappear out of sight ; twilight. *halu.*

halungigi, to overlap. *halu.*

veihalungigi, to be out of joint, dislocated.

halutinathagi, to be skilful, wise : *koda tango halutinathagigna*, be skilful in your working.

haluvagi githathagi, dusk. *halu* ; *githatha.*

hamutagi(ni) v.t. to refuse, reject. (*hauhamutagi*).

hanu, thing : *a hanu*, the person, he who ; *sa hanu*, no one, with negative. Fl. *hanu* ; R. *sanu* ; New Hebrides *hano, hen, sanu.*

hangana(gna), path, way : *base hangana*, cross-roads.

hanga, to be open. M. *wanga* ; S. *anga.*

hangavi v.t., to open, of door, box, etc. Fl. *hangavi.*

hangavia adj., opened.

hangaviagna gerund.

hangava, a fathom, the arms opened wide ; to open the arms wide. *hanga.* Fl. *hangava.*

hangavulu, numeral, ten ; not used of ' twenty ', or of units of twenty, *tutugu* being used instead. S. *tangahulu.*

haohaova, to be open.

hapara, to wear a perineal bandage.

hapi, to eat the betel-mixture.

haraihi v.t., to weed a garden.

haranggano, to grope with the hands.

harapada v.t., to meet, encounter, overtake. *pada.*

harapadagi v.t., to meet.

veiharapadagi, to encounter, meet.

hati v.t., to take, receive, marry, of man : *hati mai*, to bring ; *hati tavoga*, to remove.

hatiagna gerund.

hatha 1, to sweep, brush, a broom, clean up. R. *saasara* ; M. *sarav.* (*haahatha*).

hathagna gerund.

hatha 2 : *na mane hatha i valau*, a smith.

hathangato, a prickly weed.

hathangatu, hundred : *si na hathangatu*, a hundred. Fl. *hangalatu.*

hathautu(gna), a way. S. *hala* ; Fl. *halautu.*

hathavu v.t., to cross over, to lay across : *soni hathavu*, to make a free gift ; grace (late). Fl. *halavu.*

hathavungi v.t., to cross over.

vahathavu v.t., to hand down by tradition : *vahathavu hagore*, to interpret, act as interpreter.

hathe v.t., to help, assist. Fl. *have.*

hatheagna gerund.

veihaehathegi, to help one another.

hatho : *hatho gneku*, to build a nest ; *haohatho*, to gather, reap.

hatho ngguanggura, a tempest.

hau, to be far, a long time : *i hau*, far, of old ; *e hau me hau*, for ever and ever ; *bongi hau gohi*, it is late. M. *sau.*

haulagi, to be old, of old, before.

hauni v.t., to be far off from, distant.

haugna gerund. : *kena bosi haugna*, they were not far off.

hava interrog. pron., what ? Used also as indefinite, whatever, anything : *na hava*, what ? *bali hava*, thing for what ? why ? don't care ! *e hava*, what ? *hava nia*, how ? *e hava na*, why ? *e hava e ania*, how ? *o hava nia, e hava o ania*, how are you ? *e hava rae toke*, how good ! *na hava rae tinoni thaba*, what a great man ! *na fata hava*, what ? *na hava gua*, what else, of course ! M. *sava.*

havagini v.t., to leave a thing behind, forget.

have v.t., to roof in, thatch, a house. Fl. *have* ; S. *tahera'i.*

haveri v.t., to wear over the shoulder, as a bag. S. *taheri* ; V. *saveri.*

havi, to live, be well, to escape, of hunted animal : *havi mathangani*, to recover from sickness ; *thehe haihavi*, danger.

havi(gna), life.

vahavi v.t., to save, heal.

vahaviagna gerund.

havo v.t., to attack a village by union of forces.

havu 1, to make an offering to a ghost.

havugagi v.t., to offer, sacrifice ; a sacrifice.

havugagiagna gerund.

havu 2, to wipe, wash. V. *savula* ; M. *savsavula.*

havula v.t.

havulagna v.n., washing.

havuli v.t., to wash ; *hauhavuli*, to sprinkle.

havulu, scallop shell.

he v.t., to give to a person. Fl. *he*.
heagna gerund.

hege(gna), alone, of own accord. *gehe*.

hego, breadfruit.

hehe(gna) 1, voice.

hehe(gna) 2, heart, mind, wish, desire : *ke boi hehegna*, it was not his wish ; *hehe i tongga*, confidence ; *vano hehe*, to desire. Fl. *hehe*.

heta, to be powerful ; strength : *hatia na heta*, to be zealous.

faheaheta v.t., to be too strong for

heuhemu(gna), lip.

hi, 1, demonstr. pron. ; has emphatic use : *ivei hi mane ari*, where is that man ? *da imanea hi tuni eri*, haply he is that person ; denotes finished action, follows a vb. : *nggovu hi*, when that was finished ; *ke vula hi*, he has come ; *toke hi*, that will do ! *hina* ; *hiri*. Lam. *higea*.

hi 2, trans. suffix to vb. : *lio*, *liohi*.

hia numeral, nine. S. *siwe*.
hiagna, ninth.

hibu, ulcer.

hidi, wall, stone wall.

higara, a bird, parakeet.

higini v.t., to smell. S. *hii*.
higiniagna gerund.
hiihigini v.t., to nuzzle, kiss.

higiti v.t., to sting, hurt. R. *sigiti* ; M. *vivtig* ; S. *hi'ito'o*.
vahigiti v.t., to cause to ache, to feel pain.

hihi, to be open.

hihinggi, to shout for joy, or in triumph.

hihovu adv., all ; follows word qualified.

hii v.t., to assent to, answer, obey ; exclam., yes ! *manihihi*.

hihiila, to be obedient, of child.

hiinggili v.t., to touch.

hiingotu, to witness an act of adultery.

hili 1, to wander.

hili 2, to transgress, violate. (*hiihili*).
hilivi v.t., to infringe, violate, to go throughout.
hiliviagna gerund.

hili kaekavelato, to commit fornication, of unmarried people. *hili* 2.

hiliga(gna), near, round : *i hiligagna*, near (it) ; *hiligai meleha*, the country round about.

hina, demonstr. pron. ; has emphatic use : *teo hina*, not that ! *da anggai hina*, do this, then ! *inau hina*, it is I ! *na* 2.

hinage(gna), generic name for canoes : *hinage vaivine*, a constellation.

hinao, coconut shell cup.

hina ota, midday, the sun overhead : *hinaota patu*, noon, *hinaota lavi*, 3 p.m. Fl. *hina gota*.

hinara, to shine, of moon, stars, fireflies, lamp ; a light. Fl. *hina*.

hiohinggo, to eat up what is left, to pick up the crumbs.

hira v.t., to rebuke, strive with. (*hiahira*).

hiragna v.n.

hirara, to quarrel.

hiri demonstr. pron., pl.; has emphatic use: *ia ani hiri*, these here. *ri*.

hirama, a stone axe.

hirivu, to be bitter.

hiro v.b., to search. (*hiohiro*).

hiroagna gerund.

veihirohirogi, to search among one another.

hiroku, a funeral feast following upon a death: *pohe i hiroku*, mourning garments.

hitagi adv., indeed, even; follows the word qualified.

hito, to copulate.

hobi 1, to pierce the ear lobe. (*hoihobi*).

hobi 2, v.t., to draw near to, approach.

hoga, to be contracted, short.

hogagini v.t., to define, set a boundary to.

vahoga v.t., to define, put bounds to.

hogatha v.t., to forbid, prevent, intervene, mediate.

hogogna, like, as: *ke hogogna*, its fellow.

hogoni v.t., to store up. M. *sogon*.

hogoniagna gerund.

hogovi v.t., to hit.

hoho(gna), forehead.

hoholo, to be dangerous, danger.

hokata, clam shell armlet. R. *hokata*.

hole, to disobey, be disobedient, contradict, be contrary.

horara, the open sea. Fl. *horara*.

horu 1, times, repeated occasions; the genitive *i* follows; used as a multiplicative: *e tolu na horu i tuturiagna*, three times of telling; *sikei vamua na horu i vanonggu* I went only once.

horu 2, to go down, fall; be content, satisfied, of mind; adv., down: *horu haihadi*, to be anxious, disturbed, downcast. Fl. *horu*.

horu(gna), fall.

horuga v.n., depth; to be deep.

horugna gerund.

horuvi v.t., to descend.

horuviagna gerund.

vahoru v.t., to take down.

horugotha, to mix, mingle.

horupe v.t., to uncover, open, of oven.

hotagi(gna), waist, middle, loins: *hotagigna*, in the midst; *ke hotagi i bongi*, midnight; *vari hotagidia*, in their midst.

hotu, to fall.

hotha, to carry, carry on a pole: *tinoni hotha*, a captive, slave. Fl. *hola*.

hoahotha, to carry; a burden.

hothati v.t., to build, of house.

vahothagini v.t., to burden.

hothoho, forest: *tinoni i hothoho*, a bushman.

hothohoga(gna), forest.

hove, to refuse, be unwilling. V. *sove*; Fl. *hove*.

hua, to dip.

huahungga, to sob.

huaragini v.t., to be contrary, of wind. Fl. *huari*; S. *suahi*.

huari v.t., to rebuke.

huati v.t., to question, ask about. Fl. *huati*.

huatiagna gerund.

veihuahuatigi, to question one another.

hugu(gna) 1, harbour. S. *su'u*.

hugu 2, to deny, dispute, be fractious, rebellious ; used with *ni* 1. Fl. *hugu*.

hugugna v.n.

veihuhugu, *veihuhugugi*, to dispute, altercate, brawl, of two people ; an altercation.

huguru, a grove, of coconuts, areca palms, sago palms, bamboos, a thicket.

huguta, to acquire sole power, of a chief, to dispossess, unseat, to be supreme ; kingdom, rule.

huguti, a sand worm.

huha, to put on, of clothing, wrap oneself up ; used with *ni* 1.

huhagna gerund., covering, wrapping.

huhasi v.t., to clothe.

huhu, chameleon.

huhuri, to fill.

huhuru adv., exceedingly, greatly, much. Fl. *huhuru*.

hui v.t., to take down, let down, cease, finish, redeem : *hui gohi na tarai*, are prayers over? Fl. *hui*.

vahuihui, last, final.

hujuu v.t., to approach, thrust, push : *hujuu mai*, to draw near to ; *hujuu hadi*, to move position ; *hujuu sapa*, to push out, launch, of canoe ; used also with *ni* 1.

hukunu v.t., to pull up, of fish in net.

hulagini v.t., to summon.

huli(gna), bone. S. *suli* ; Fl. *huli*.

hulu v.t., to lift. Fl. *hulu* ; S. *sulu*.

hulungi v.t.

hulumaruarua, to be brackish, of water.

hume, to root up ground, of pigs feeding. (*huehume*).

hunua, passage in reef, channel.

hungu, to be full, to rise, of sea, to be well fed. *vonu*. S. *hungu*.

hunguti v.t., to fill, throng, crowd round.

veihungutigi, to be crammed full.

huri v.t., to pluck up, uproot. Fl. *huri*.

huriagna gerund.

huriloka v.t., to uproot, transplant.

huru, to urge, press, push, assert : *vele huhuru*, to urge, persuade, provoke. Fl. *huru*.

huruagna gerund.

huruku, latrine.

hurupe v.t., to open, undo, of parcel.

hutu 1, to be big, great, large.

hutua adj., big, much.

vahutu v.t., to increase.

hutu(gna) 2, ancestor, parent.

huu, to sink, dive, go down, of sun : *huu davi*, to dive for pearl shell ; *na huu i aho*, *huuna aho*, sunset. S. *suu*.

I

i 1, personal article, seen in prefix to personal pronouns : *inau*, *igoe*, *igita*, etc. M. *i*.

i 2, locative preposition, at, from : *i longa, i ngiha, i jangigna*; *i kosi*; precedes place-names. Sol. Is. *i*.

i 3, genitive : *na huu i aho*, sunset ; *dathe i Sion*, daughter of Sion ; *dathe i botho*, a little pig ; used to denote purpose : *kena sopou i vanga*, they sat down to eat ; *keda boi goi vano horu i hatia*, let him not go down again to take it ; used following the verbs *turugu*, to begin ; *tabiru*, to turn into, become ; *vuha*, to become. S. *i*.

i 4, verbal suffix : *baka, bakai*; *pono, ponoi*. S. *i*.

i 5, instrumental prefix to nouns : *idathe, ignavi, ikonga, itina*. M. *i*.

i 6, suffix to numerals : *varuai*, second.

ia demonstr. pronoun : *ia ani*; *ia eni*; *ia vamua eni*, that is it !

iaani demonstr. pronoun, this, here ; follows a noun.

iaeni demonstr. pronoun, this ; follows a noun.

ianggeri demonstr. pronoun, that, there : *ianggeri ari*, that's it ! *sikei ianggeri, sikei ianggeri*, that's one thing, that's another.

iangeni demonstr. pronoun, that, there, thus ; follows a noun.

idathe, stone used in hand in cracking canarium almonds. *dathe. itina*.

ido(gna), mother, mother's sister : *idogna na liva*, centipede ; *ido i meleha*, mother of countries ! exclam. of astonishment.

ifu v.t., to blow, of fire or pan-pipes, to light, of fire or lamp ; panpipes. S. *uhi*. (*ifuifu*).

ifuagna, gerund.

iga, fish ; imported word.

igami, we (excl.).

igamu, you.

igita, we (incl.).

igoe, thou.

ihu(gna), nose, beak. Fl., R. *ihu*.

iia, she. *iira*.

iini v.t., to make scratches on, incise, mark. S. *iini*.

iira they, used of women only : *ro iira na vaivine*, the two women. *iia*.

iju, to count : *iju vathe*, to go from house to house, gad about. Fl., S. *idu*. (*ijuiju*).

ijumi, v.t., to count, read.

ijumia v.n., counting, number. *ijumiagna*, gerund.

i ke anggai eni adv., now.

ikonga, a crook for detaching fruit, etc., *i* 5.

i kenugua, to-day. *kenugua*.

i kosi adv., within. *kosi*.

ikosigna, within, inside.

iku, vocative, younger brother or sister.

inggai adv., until, the time preceding an event ; precedes a vb. : *e vati mua na magavu inggai nggi u taviti*, there are four days before I go.

ili, to totter, oscillate : *nia ili na hiroagna*, to search diligently ; *kou ili*, to be drunken. (*iliili*).

ilonga, landwards from sea, on shore. *longa*.

imanea, he. *mane*.

imaraira, they, of persons or things ; *imaraira ani*, these. *mara*.

imarea, they, of persons.

inau, I. M. *inau*.

ingiha adv., when ? how long ? Fl. id.

ignavi, tongs ; to take up with tongs. *i* 5.

igne, to be red hot.

ignotha, yesterday. S. *i nonola*.

iraani these.

iraeni, these.

irangeni, those.

irogami, we two (excl.).

irogamu, you two.

irgiota, we two (incl.).

iroira, they two.

iromaraira, they two.

iru(gna), ear ; to enter the ear, of words, dirt, insect, etc. : *iru pono*, closed ears, bold, fearless.

isi(gna), sword. Fl. *isi*. Apparently an imported word.

isile, to tattoo a woman's face, cutting it and rubbing in lime.

iso, to be small, little, few.
  isoa adj., small, little.
  vaiso, few.
  vaisoa adj., few.

ita prep., among, from, by ; the pronouns of possession are always suffixed : *itagna na maiagna mai*, at his coming : *ke sabiri itanggua*, he bought it from me ; *na kuli itadia*, they have ears. *ta* 1.

itaba, on shore. *taba*.

itina, the understone used in cracking canarium almonds. *i* 5 ; *idathe*. Fl. *tina*, mother.

itolugami, we three (excl.).

itolugamu, you three.

itolugita, we three (incl.).

ituitu v.t., to cover in the oven with leaves and hot stones.

iu onomatop., dog : *mane iuiu*, a vagabond, loafer.

iuigu(gna), tail, of dog, bird, fish. Fl. *igu* ; S. *ʻuʻiʻuʻi*.

iva(gna), brother- or sister-in-law. U. *iha*.

ivei adv., where ? how ? place where, anywhere : *ivei mivei*, wheresoever, everywhere ; *ivei ke ania*, how ? *ivei mai*, whence ? *iveimu*, what part of you ? *vei*. U. *ihei*.

J

jae, estuary, mouth of stream.
  jaejae, to spear fish along an estuary.

jagimaha, ship, iron.   *maha*. V. *jahimaha*. *tapalao*.

jai v.t., to pierce.

jalakulu, to be troubled in mind, perplexed, in doubt as to procedure.

jangigna : *i jangigna*, formerly. Fl. *idania*.

jao 1, forest.

jao 2, small oblong fishing net with short handle.

japu, square fishing net tied at the four corners to two bent canes, with long handle.

jaraha, fishing net ten fathoms long, drawn between two canoes.

jari(gna), a watercourse, dug channel, passage in reef ; to make or mend a passage or path ; *jarigna na bea*, bed of the river. S. *dari*.

jaijari, a natural channel.

jata 1, to be brimful, fullness.

jatangagi v.t., to be brimful of.

jata 2, flood tide : *na jata i obo*, high tide.

jatavi v.t., to meet, encounter, go to meet.

jataviagna gerund.

jathe v.t., to call, cry out, call out to, summon, be reconciled to. (*jaejathe*).

jatheagna gerund.

jathegi v.t., to hail, call out to.

veijathegi, to be reconciled to one another, make amends mutually.

jau, fishing net, generic term ; to catch fish with a net.

jaura, to surround, enmesh.

jautovu, to prosper, flourish, increase, be in abundance ; n., increase, abundance : *havi jautovu*, to be in good health ; *jautovugna*, its increase. *tovu*.

jefe, to stray, go out of the way, wander, to make a mistake in speech. (*jeejefe*).

jefehagini v.t., to turn away from.

vajefe v.t., to deceive, mislead.

jefira, to slip, slide.

jemi, canoe paddle, generic term.

jeujemuru, fringe of object, hem, border.

jiijigi, to take an oath, swear by ; n., oath : *jiijigi Soga*, by Soga ! *jiijigi idonggu*, by my mother ! *jiijigi kabi*, to swear falsely.

jike, to avoid, shun, out of fear or respect ; used with *ni* 1 :

jike sani, to turn aside from, be afraid of ; *jiejike*, to respect, show reverence for, fear.

jikehagini v.t., to turn aside from, avoid.

jino, to be straight, right, righteous (late).

jinoa adj., straight, right.

vajino v.t., to make straight, guide, justify.

jirijoro, ornamented belt.

joijongi v.t., to importune ; adv., persistently, importunately ; follows a vb. : *turu joijongi*, to be very filthy.

jolo, to be wounded.

jongo, to be black ; blackness : *jongogna*, its blackness.

jororo, to slip, slide.

joto, fire.

jotha : *horu jotha*, to mix.

joajotha, to be mixed, of colours, or of people from various villages : *hagore joajotha*, to speak various languages.

vajoajotha v.t., to confuse.

veijothavigi, to intermingle, be confused, confusion.

jou 1, v.t., to dig a hole, to plant ; a plant.

jou 2, v.t., to hew, carve.

joujou, to hollow out wooden or stone bowls.

jovo, to be deceived.

vajovo v.t., to deceive.

veijovogi, to deceive one another.

jufu, to arrive, reach ; arrival.

jufungi v.t., to reach, arrive at.

juka, to be equal, to yoke together, weigh (late), exchange, lend, borrow, of money : *juajuka*, to compare, used with *ni* 1 ; *juajuka tomaga*, to

obtain interest on money lent ;
bali juka, a yoke ; *juajuka*,
weighing scales.

veijukagi, to dispute with, argue.

juloto, to be perverse, contrary.

juru v.t., to burn, kindle. *pugujuru*.

juruagna gerund.

juta, torch, lamp, candle.

jutu, to approach, draw near to.
jutuvi v.t.

juujuku v.t., to strike, hurt, harm,
be cruel to.

Ch

The sound of *ch* is as *ch* in
English ' church '.

chagao, frog.

chapo v.t., to wash, drawing an
article to and fro in water.
chapoagna gerund.

cheche, grasshopper.

cheu 1, coconut bottle, well, cup.
seu.

cheu 2, to refresh.

chiu v.t., to enter into.

chogo, corner post of house,
corner.

choachoma, on tiptoe : *teteri choachoma*, to stand on tiptoe.

choku, to poke.

chuchuru, to prick, stick into.

chuu v.t., to drive.

K

ka adjectival prefix : *kamoto*. S.
'a. Fl. *ka*.

kaa, a drain. Fl. *kaa*.

kaakata, to ram, of earth.

kabauli, to be unequal in length
or height.

kabesau v.t., to gird oneself with
a cloth. Fl. *kabe*.

kabi : *jiijigi kabi*, to swear falsely.

kabili, to bite.

kabokili v.t., to entrust.

kabolagini v.t., to draw together,
of strands in plaiting.

kado, a joint : *kado i huli*, a
cubit.

kadolulu, a section of bamboo,
water vessel. *kado*.

kae v.t., to beseech, beg, ask for :
kae togokale, to implore.
kaeagna gerund.

kaekafe v.t., to store up ; a
treasure, heirloom.
kaekafeagna gerund.

kaekale v.t., to search, spy out,
watch.
kaekaleagna gerund.

kaekane v.t., to aim at, point out.
fakane ; kene.

kaekave, to be old, of woman.
kave.

kaekavelato, a maiden : *havi kaekavelato*, a bastard.

kaekavere, a spider. Fl. *kaekavere*.

kafa, to whittle.

kago v.t., to husk a coconut :
kago niu. Fl. *kago*.

kaikahi v.t., to shake, move
about : *gaigali kaikahi*, to
rock oneself to and fro. Fl.
kahi.
kahiagna gerund.

kaja, a storm.

kajari, to cut, cut off, carve.

kajiga, to cough ; a cough.
gajika.

kaju v.t., to make, build, of canoe,
to carve. (*kakaju*).
kajuagna gerund.

kaka vocative, elder brother or
sister.

kakaba, shoal water.

kakabakeha, accursed, devoted, charmed.

kakai, to be firm, steady, faithful, right : *na tinoni kakai*, an upright, honest man. Fl. *kakai*.

kakamo, a measure, handbreath, span.

kakango, to dry up.

kakava, to be dried up, parched, of ground.

kakau, crab. Fl. *kakau*.

kake, taro. Fl. *kake*.

kakega adj., uncooked, raw, of pudding.

kanggiri, to be stingy, grudging.

kanggu, to creep, crawl. Fl. *langgu*. (*kaukanggu*).

kangguli v.t., to climb, creep along, to go secretly after a woman.

kalabae, to be paralysed.

kalai, reef, shoal : *ke sapa na kalai*, ebb tide ; *ke paa na kalai*, low tide.

kalasu : *kalasu mai*, to come ; *kalasu atu*, to go away.

kaliti v.t., to tend, guard, prepare. (*kaikaliti*).

kalitiagna gerund.

kama, to be big : *manu kama*, sea eagle ; *kama nago*, the firstborn. Fl. *kama*.

kamane(gna), companion, fellow, kinsfolk ; to company with, be opposite to, over against : *kamanemu*, along with you. V. *kama*.

kamoto adj., cut off, broken off short. *ka* 1. M. *mot*, broken off. (*kaokamoto*).

kamotoa adj., *id*.

kana enemy : *ninggua na kana*, my enemy. R., Fl. *kana* ; V. *kanali*.

kanalagi, persecution.

kanalagini v.t., to molest, be inimical to.

kagnu v.t., to shake, of earthquake, to shake off. *agnu*. V. *kakanu*. (*kaukagnu*).

kaokanggo, a coconut, one stage.

kapa, semen.

kapi v.t., to lop off, strip off, amputate. Fl. *kapi*.

kapisa, to be narrow. Fl. *kapi*.

kapoti, a crab.

kaputi v.t., to fix, erect, set up, establish. Fl. *kaputi*.

kaputiagna gerund.

kara, to be barren, of women.

karango, reef : *ke paa na karango*, low tide. Fl. *karango*.

kari 1, conj., but ; serves as a connective.

kari 2, to scrape, of flesh of coconut, rasp. M. *gar*, Fl. *kari*, wipe. (*kakari*).

karu, thorn. S. *karu*, clutch. (*kaukaru*).

kasa 1, sea eel.

kasa 2, to be complete, of counting, to be fulfilled, of words, to be paid in full, of debt : *e salage kasa*, a full ten : *na ijumi kasagamugna*, to number you in full.

kasagna v.n., fulfilment.

vakasa v.t., to fulfil : *vakasa magavu*, a funeral feast at month's end after a death.

vakasagna v.n., fulfilment, completion.

kasapa, a booth. *sakapa*.

kasie, a bat.

kasila, the spleen.

kaso, comfort, consolation.

vakaso v.t., to comfort.

kati pronominal verbal particle, 1st pers. pl. incl., we. *ati.*

kato(gna), cave in coral reef, hole, the anus, eye of needle.

katura(gna), a seed.

katha, hair-comb ; to comb the hair. Fl. *kavakava.*

kathe v.t., to hit, strike.   Fl. *kale.*

kaekathe v.t., to afflict, trouble ; n., agony, trouble, plague.

vakathe v.t., to establish, confirm, to fall upon, of trouble.

kau, to be caught, hung up, entangled. Fl., U. *kau.*

kaukalu v.t., to stir up, knead with the hands. M. *kal.*

kaukau(gna), finger, toe : *kaukau i lima*, finger ; *kaukau i nae*, toe.

kaupuru v.t., to swarm over, of maggots, worms.

kavali, south-east squall.   Fl. *kavali.*

kavali aara, south-east wind. *aara.*

kavaligi, to lean, to decline, of sun ; a division of the day, late afternoon. *ligi.*

kave(gna), grandmother. *kaekave.*

kavelu, to turn, turn away, revolve ; time of day, 2 p.m. : *kavelu sani*, to forsake.

kavena, to watch, guard ; a watch. (*kaekavena*).

kavuhi v.t., to shake, shake down nuts, to winnow, shake off. Fl. *kavuhi.*

kavuku onomatop., pigeon.

kavuvu, to cast fruit prematurely, to abort.

ke v.p., without tense significance ; used with the gerundives and with certain noun forms : *ke nabamu*, sufficient for you ; *ke kenegna*, opposite it ; *ke tonogna*, his possessions ; *ke dikatagna*, he was angry ; used with adjectives : *ke hutu*, large ; *na vathe ke tabu*, the sanctuary ; combines with the pronominal verbal particles *ati, iti, oti, ena*, and also with the pronouns *u, o*, the vowel *e* being dropped, *kati, ku*, etc.

kea 1, demonstr. pron., that ; follows a noun ; used also as personal pron., 3rd sing., he.

kea(gna) 2, rump, bottom, underpart.

keakera(gna), ankle.

ke anggai eni adv., now. *anggai.*

keana conj., but, nevertheless. *kea* 1.

kebihagi v.t., to hate.

veikekebi, to hate one another.

keda 1, pronominal verbal particle, 3rd pers. sing. used of future, he will, it will. *da* 1.

keda 2, a canoe, seating five ; raised stern.

kedana as *keda* 1, but used of 3rd pers. pl., they will.

keha, numeral, one, in a series. Fl. *keha.*

kei 1, round basket made of coconut leaf. Fl. *kei.*

kei(gna) 2, tooth.

keju, earthworm. Fl. *kedu.* V. *kezu.*

keke exclam., eh ! of pain or fear ; to cry out, to say *keke.*

kekelagini v.t., to cry out at a person, to ask, importune.

kekeha indefinite pron., pl., certain ; precedes noun. *keha.*

kekeve, glass beads. Fl., R. *kekeve* ; L. *kekefe.*

kemuli v.t., to distribute.
keukemu, to be generous : *ni keukemu,* to distribute.
keukemuliagna gerund.

kena pronominal verbal particle, 3rd pers. pl., they. *ena.*

kenada, as *kedana.*

kene 1, to point, aim. *kaekane.* Fl. *kene,* seek. (*keekene*).

kene 2, to be opposite, over against, to be contrary : *ke kenegna,* over against, opposite to.

kenugua, to-day, by and by, presently : *kenugua vuovugoi* (*vuevugei*), to-morrow morning.

kepi, eyeshade, hat. Fl. *kepi.*

keru, lime ; v.t., to lime the hair, etc.
keruagna gerund.

kethe(*gna*), the vagina.

keukevu, to annoy, irritate, worry.

ki trans. suffix to vb. : *piru, piruki.*

kia, to laugh. V., Fl. *kia.* (*kiakia*).
kiagi v.t., *kiahagi*(*ni*) v.t., *kiakiagini* v.t., to laugh at.

kiakuku, to chuckle. *kia.*

kiakidapu, to warm oneself in the sun.

kiala, canoe house. Fl. *kiala.*

kiari v.t., to drag, draw.

kiba, pawpaw.

kibo, debt. V. *kibo.*

kidi, for the first time, formerly, before ; precedes a vb. Fl. *diki.*

kidiri, to be lowering, overcast, of sky.

kidoru(*gna*), egg : *kidoru i mata,* apple of the eye ; *kidoru i davi,* a pearl.

kiekigne, a green parrot.

kiekile, a tomahawk set on a long handle, for fighting. S. *kilekile.*

kiikidi, to rap, knock with the knuckles. Fl. *kidi.*

kiki 1, to be little. Fl. *kiki.*

kiki 2, to be slow. Fl. *kiki.*

kikii, to scratch. L. *kiikii,* rat.

kikiri, to be little. *kiki* 1.

kikimua adv., presently, by and by, gently, slowly. *kiki* 2.

kikirase, a harlot.

kikitiri, to be bold, to dare, do with determination.

kikituru, a night-bird.

kinggulu, musical instrument with two strings. V. *tunggulu.*

kilahi, to sulk.
kiakilahi, to begrudge.

kilili v.t., to be round about, around : *tabo kilili,* to grope ; *taviti kilili,* to walk about. Fl. *kilili.*
kililia adj., round about.
kililiagna gerund., around.
kiligna v.n., encompassing.

kilionggu, a pool.

kilo 1, v.t., to call : *kilo meemee, kilo hahali,* to importune ; *kilo au,* ecclesia, the Church. (*kiokilo*).
kiloagna gerund.
veikilokilogi, to call one another.

kilo 2, hole in the ground.

kignibi, to pinch. M. *gin* ; S. *ini.*

kio, to kick.

kiokido, to beat a drum, to chatter, of teeth ; a drum.

kiokilo, an ulcer.

kiri 1, v.t., to bind, wrap.

kiriagna gerund.

kiri(gna) 2, corpse.

kirio, porpoise. S. *'irio*.

kisu, to be struck with a curse. Fl. *kisu*.

kiti pronominal verbal particle, we (excl.). *iti*.

kiukisu, vegetable mash ; to mash taros, yams, etc.

ko pronominal verbal particle, thou. *o*.

koakoa 1, fornication, sin ; to sin.

koakoa 2 : *koakoa i hagetha*, sill of door.

koakoha, to be bare, bald.

koakota i mata, eyelid.

koba 1, to be destitute, void, empty. Fl. *koba*.

kobathagi, to be bare, destitute.

kobathagini v.t., to strip off, strip bare.

koba 2, the hermit crab. *koba* 1. R., Fl. *koba*.

kobili, a large fish, groper.

koburu, N.W. wind. Fl. *koburu*.

kobusa, mature, of fruit, but unripe.

kodili, musical instrument with one string.

kodo 1, to carry, of file of men in pairs carrying a log. Fl. *kodo*.

kodo 2, to be crippled, maimed ; a cripple.

kodoko, to paddle.

koi, noun of assemblage, used as pl. article of persons ; precedes noun : *na koi tinoni*, men ; *koi vaivine*, you women ! *komi*.

koiliu, backwards and forwards, about : *taviti koiliu*, to walk about ; *hagore koiliu*, to speak in a parable. *liu*. (*koikoiliu*).

koilo, dwarf coconut, with yellow fruit.

koki, to be sorrowful, miserable, confined to house through illness.

kokiroko onomatop., to crow, of cock ; a cock.

koko 1, v.t., to store, lay up.

koko 2, wooden gong. S. *'o'o* ; Fl. *koko*.

kokoilo : *kutu kokoilo*, stomach.

kokoju, to clip the hair short.

kokolagi, an offering to a ghost, not food.

kokolo, blue, of stalactite.

kokomo, shell of coconut.

kokopa(gna), ridge of house. Fl. *kokopa*.

kokopono, to be thick, of weather, foggy, mist. *pono*.

kokcto, edge, end, beginning, foundation of wall, bottom of bowl inside : *kokoto i maha*, bottom of the sea.

kokou, stem of tobacco pipe.

kongga 1, to gag a pig with a stick ; a gag, bit : *kongga baabara*, the lintel of a door, the transverse beam above the door.

konggulagini v.t., to gag, bridle.

kongga 2, a grove of areca palms. *tootoo*. Fl. *kongga*.

konggana, an ornamental shield.

konggoro, a wooden peg used in house-building, an arrow tipped with bone.

konggu 1, wild ginger.

konggu 2, to lead.

konggulagini v.t., to lead, guide,

teach a child to walk, holding it under the arms, to assist a sick person to walk.

kola(gna), the liver : *ke vuivui na kolagna*, his liver swings, i.e. he is in mortal terror.

kolagna : *hagore kolagna*, to guess, conjecture : vain talking ; *hai kolagna*, to be in vain.

koli, to lie down, lie : *koli pogo*, to lie upon the face, capsize, of canoe ; *na bali koligna*, that on which he lay. Fl. *koli*.

vakoli v.t., to cause to lie down, to bury.

kolili adv., about, around. *lili*. Fl. *kolili*.

kolo, pool, lake : *kolo papauro*, the legendary lake over which souls pass to Bolofaginia, the Lord of the dead. *kotho*. R. *kolo* ; Fl. *kolo*, water.

kololo, the coconut beetle ; to be worm-eaten, hollow-eyed. Fl. *kololo*.

kome(gna), tusk.

komi noun of assemblage, used as pl. article of persons and things ; precedes a noun : *na komi tinoni*, men ; *na komi fata*, things. *koi*. IN. Roro, *ikoi* ; Duke of York, *kum* ; M. *numwei, ML.* 231.

kono, sorrow, grief.

kookono, to mourn ; grief, sorrow.

kongati v.t., to cut off, reap. *kongatiagna* gerund.

kongo, toucan.

kongo, large black ant.

kopi 1, the boatbill heron.

kopi 2, reddish in colour.

kora(gna), inside, within, in, at : *koranggu inau*, in me ; the locative *i* may be prefixed : *i koragna*, within, in. *kori*.

korangasa(gna), brain, marrow : *korangasa i suli*, marrow.

kore, filthy, unclean (late).

kori prep., within, in, at, of, from, into : *kori vathe*, in the house ; *rugu au kori*, to go out from. *kora + i* 2.

koro pronominal verbal particle, you two, they two.

koroga, to be apart, separate, desolate, deserted, of persons : *koroga sani*, to depart from.

korongohu(gna), skull.

kosi, outside, without : *i kosigna*, outside. *i kosi*.

koti pronominal verbal particle, you.

koto v.t., to shave the top of the head, clip hair.

kotolu pronominal verbal particle, you three.

kotu, to spring up, of plants, grow, ascend. Fl. *kotu*.

vakotu v.t., to cause to grow.

kotho, oil, liquid : *kotho i mata*, tears ; *kotho nggoenggoe*, lukewarm. *kolo*.

kothobu i mata, tears. *kotho*. Fl. *kolobu*, dew.

kou v.i., to drink : *na bali kou*, water to drink ; a drinking vessel.

kouvi v.t., to drink. L. *gwou*. *kouviagna* gerund.

vakou(vi) v.t., to cause to drink, to water animals.

koukovuru, embers, coals. Fl. *gougovu*.

kovesa, mist, vapour.

kovihoho, snail.

kovotho : *vanga kovotho*, to pilfer food.

ku pronominal verbal particle, I. *u.*

kuakuala, to cry out, call.

kuali, bird arrow, of rib of sago palm leaf. Fl. *kuali*.

kudo, to be short, not tall, low.
  kudoa adj., short.
  kudohagini v.t., to come short of.
  vakudo v.t., to shorten.

kue(gna), old man, an elder, ancestor, old age. Fl. *kukua*.

kuhi, rat. Fl. *kuhi*.

kuikuli, frog.

kuikuji, barbed, of arrow, etc.

kuikurigi, to strip.

kuikuvi v.t., to cover. Fl. *kuvi*. V. *kovi*.
  kuikuviagna gerund.

kujikaru, a thorny creeper. *karu.*

kujuku(gna), end, tip.
  kujukui, to be the last.

kuchachi, earwig.

kukigni, trouble, anguish.

kuku : *kia kuku*, to chuckle.

kukua(gna), grandfather, grand-child, ancestor, descendant. Fl. *kukua*.

kukubo v.t., to uproot.

kukuro, thunder, a gun : *thehe kukuro* to die suddenly. Fl. *kukuro*.

kula(gna), friend : *kulanggu* voc., friend ! Fl. *kula*.
  kulaga v.n., friendship.

kulau, a tree frog.

kuleru, a bamboo pipe with two notes.

kuli(gnu) 1, ear, corner of object, fin of fish. Fl. *kuli*.

kuli 2, to pluck, of fruit.

kuma, to be poor, needy, destitute ; poverty.

kumusi, to fade, be faded.

kuna, to strain, of exertion, women in labour. *pete kuna.*

kuokuo i gai, a rod.

kupape, to be sleepy.

kupi, maiden, bachelor : *na kupi vaivine*, a maiden.

kupo, grasshopper.

kuri, coral.

kurijelu(gna), heart.

kuro, to boil in a saucepan.

kurohu, green coconut, in drinkable stage.

kuru pronominal verbal particle, we two (excl.).

kusu : *tara kusu*, *vuru kusu*, to cut off.

kutolu pronominal verbal particle, we three (excl.).

kutu(gna) 1, belly, womb, heart. Fl. *kutu*.

kutu 2, to fall down. Fl. *kutu*.
  kutugna v.n., a fall.
  kutuvi v.t., to fall upon.
  vakutuli v.t., to abort, of pig.

kutumaedu, to reel, stagger. *kutu* 2.

kuufa, a smell, pungent odour : *kuufa paraguha*, an unpleasant smell.

kuukumu, to be dull, overcast, of sky.

kuukunu, to plot, meditate evil.

kuukuu onomatop., pigeon.

kuumeemere, to look sad.

kuvuri v.t., to cover over, bury, hide.
  kuvuriagna gerund.

Ngg

The sound of *ngg* is that of *ng* in 'finger'; *ngg* is a change from *k*.

nggaenggarere to crackle, as dead leaves, or of fire spreading.

nggahili, white cockatoo.

ngganggaru, to itch, scratch. U. *karu*, skin disease, to scratch. *nggarusi* v.t., to scratch.

nggama, hard black stone : *patu nggama*, hard, of heart. Fl. *gama*, quartz pebble.

nggarangguma, a palm.

nggari(gna), child, used of children up to five or six years old : *nggari mane*, boy; *nggari vaivine*, girl; *nggari baso*, a twin ; *ei nggari*, to have a child ; *nggaringgu*, my youth. Fl. *nggari*.

fanggainggari, to act as a child.

nggaratu, a spear.

nggaru, to be dirty, filthy, mouldy.

ngge conj., has consequential meaning, then, thereupon, after that ; not used with a subject ; the vowel of *ngge* drops before the pronouns *u*, I, *o*, thou ; also before the v.p. *ati*, *iti*, *oti*, *ena*, etc. ; may be followed by *minggoi*, lest. Fl. *ngge*.

nggenggefe, the flying fox.

nggeni, to-day, of time past, already, just now. Fl. *nggeni*.

nggeo, tide rip ; to get up, of sea.

nggeno, to be disorderly, of crowd, disturbed.

nggeonggeno, to disturb, vex ; disorder.

nggeri demonstr. pron., that, those ; there ; follows a noun. *ianggeri*.

nggenggeri, there.

nggetu, to wave from side to side, wag, move, of leaves.

nggeunggevuga, to be covetous ; covetousness.

nggi conj., has illative force, ' in consequence'; also connective, thereupon, then, and ; used with v.p. *e*, meaning ' if ', ' in order that ', ' to ' ; denotes ' that ' in dependent clauses ; used of indirect speech ; may be followed by *minggoi*, lest.

ngginggi v.t., to drive off.

nggilu v.t., to bury : *nggiunggi-lugna*, his burial. Fl. *nggilu*. S. *kilu*, hole.

nggiunggiluagna gerund.

nggina, to torment, chastise, punish.

vanggina v.t.

nggipo, to be occupied with, busy, to work hard ; used with *ni* 1. Fl. *pipo*.

nggiri, to rub, saw, with motion to and fro : *nggiri kei*, to gnash the teeth. Fl. *nggi-nggiri*.

nggoenggoe, to groan.

nggoenggothe, a wrinkle.

nggofe, spider.

nggoinggoni, to lay waste, make desolate : *talu hai nggoinggoni*, to lay waste.

nggola, to be bruised ; a bruise.

nggolu, to eat human flesh.

nggomo, to be tender.

nggotihi v.t., to break. Fl. *nggoti*, (*nggoinggotihi*).

nggotihiagna gerund.

nggovu, finished, completed : *nggovu hi*, then, thereupon, that is finished ! *na veihaohagoregi nggovuagna*, to finish the conversation. Fl. *nggovu*.

nggounggovu, all, whole, complete, finished ; follows a verb.

vanggovu v.t., to finish, complete : *vanggovugna*, the last, end, finish.

nggou, to be uninhabited, of place, deserted and overgrown. V. *nggou*.

nggu suffixed pron. of possession, my.

nggua as *nggu*; added to *ga* 1, *ni* 2.

ngguanggura, to prepare food by stone-boiling, to bubble, as when a stone is dropped into the water. *buaburara* ; *pachangguanggura*. Fl. *ngguanggura*.

nggunggu : *aliali nggunggu*, to be disturbed in mind, troubled.

nggungguru, grass.

nggungguvi v.t., to throng, press upon, of crowd.

nggungguvu, to be heavy.

ngguluva, to faint from hunger, to be very hungry ; hunger.

nggumao, to be mean, stingy.

nggumu, thunder. *tanggumu*. Fl. *nggumu*.

nggumunggeu v.t., to roar, of thunder.

ngguunggululu, to make a loud noise, roar, of water or wind ; a loud noise, roar.

ngguunggumu v.t., to chew, meditate upon.

ngguunggunu onomatop., to grumble.

ngguungguu onomatop., to mutter.

L

la trans. suffix to vb. : *diadikala* ; *boiboila* ; *havula*. Fl. *la*.

laalaba, yard, open space in front of house. L. *laba*.

laalaka(gna), throat.

laba, to reach, arrive : *lalaba tagna*, to reach him.

labangi v.t.

labutao v.t., to hang or lay across, as clothes on a line, to saddle. *tao*.

lae, to be weak, infirm.

laema, light, illumination ; to be illuminated.

valaema v.t., to give light to, illuminate.

lafi v.t., to sear.

lagagna verbal noun suffix : *diadikalagna* ; *toetokelagna*.

lagi verbal suffix : *tau, taulagi*. Fl. *lagi*.

lagini trans. suffix to vb. : *keke, kekelagini*.

lago, cone shell, ornament of cone shell. S. *la'o*.

lakiti, a scented shrub.

laku v.t., to catch, seize. *langgu*. *lakuagna* gerund.

langgo : *sono langgo*, to swallow whole. U. *laku*, whole.

langgu v.t., to carry off by force, despoil, use despitefully. L. *lagu*. (*laulanggu*).

lalahi, cross-bar of door for fastening : *bilaki lalahi*, to shut up.

lalauhe, mosquito net.

lali(gna), buttress of tree. L. *lali*, root.

langasa, to be thirsty ; thirst.

lange(gna), forehead : *teo na lange*, impudent, witless.

laolako v.t., to carry on the shoulder, of a number of men. *laolakoagna* gerund.

vaulaolako, to carry a canoe on cross sticks.

laolaomanga, haughtily, insolently.

lapa, bowl, shallow vessel. V. *lapa*.

lasa : *hai lasa*, wantonly.

lau, beach, seashore, seaward, south. *i lau*. M. *lau*.

laubano, close by, near, next to.

laulahu, to play, sport, of children.

lau saba, careless : *hai tango lau sasaba*, to work carelessly ; *lau sasaba*, to despise, think lightly of ; adv., carelessly, heedlessly : *hagore lau sasaba*, flippant talk.

laulamu, to caulk canoe with *tita*.

laulau, washboard of canoe.

lavi, evening : *ke lavi*, in the evening. U. *saulahi* ; M. *ravrav*.

lavo, haze, vapour ; to be misty, hazy. Fl. *lavo*.

lealeaa, to be joyful, glad, to rejoice.

lee, to no purpose : *hai pagana lee*, in vain. Fl. *lee*, merely.

leea adv., freely, at no cost.

lebi, to separate, part, to push aside branches in one's way : *butuli lelebi*, to tread down out of the way.

leelehe, plague, pestilence.

leeleve, sideways, askance : *doodoro leeleve*, to look askance, be envious. R. *kevekeve*.

legu v.t., to follow ; adv., after, behind : *legu vahui*, at last, the last thing in a row ;

nggari legu, younger child ; *talu legu*, to humble oneself ; *leulegu magavu*, daily ; *leulegu tinoni*, every man.

legugna, after, next, alongside ; a descendant : *i legugna*, afterwards.

leguagna gerund., according to.

lekona, native tobacco. Fl. *lekona*.

lelegai, garden. Fl. *legai*.

lelegia, mangrove.

leo, law. Lam. *leo*.

leuleu v.t., to mock, make a jest of. *theuthehu*.

li trans. suffix to vb. : *butu, butuli*. Fl. *li*.

liboro v.t., to gather almond nuts, to harvest ; harvest.

liborogna, v.n.

ligi, to incline, drop the head. M. *ling* ; Fl. *ligi*.

liligi, to oscillate, wobble, capsize, of canoe, wag, of head.

valigi v.t., to incline, lean, cause to wobble.

ligi mero, to wag the head. *ligi*.

valigimero v.t., to turn away, of face.

ligo v.t., to strangle, to strangle oneself. S. *li'o*.

vaivaligo v.t., to choke, strangle, wrestle.

linggomo, a ghost connected with war. R. *linggomo*.

lilama, uninhabited place, wilderness.

lilihi, to go, go to and fro, to coast along : *taviti lilihi*, to go by sea, not by land. Fl. *lilihi* ; S. *lili*. (*liililihi*).

lima(gna) 1, hand, wing : *tataba i lima*, palm of hand ; *matha i lima*, handiwork. Fl. *lima*.

D

lima 2, numeral, five.   *lima* 1.
   limagna, fifth.
   valima, five times.
lio(gna), heart, mind, desire, will :
   lio sikei, determined, resolute,
   to be of one mind : *tahotha
   lio*, jealous.   Fl. *lio*.
liohi v.t., to look at.   U. *lio*.
lioliko, to be crooked, winding,
   up and down, of path.
liolino, to walk about, perambu-
   late.
liu v.t., to go beyond, pass.   S.
   liu.
   liungi v.t. ; *saki liungi*, to step
   over.
   liusagini v.t., to exceed, go
   beyond.
   valiu v.t., to spread.
liuleva, to flourish, grow freely,
   of plants ; adv. freely.   *liu*.
liulivu, to give, make a gift ;
   a gift, pledge of fellowship.
   Cf. Fl. *liulivuti*.
liutuu v.t., to dam, to be enclosed,
   shut up.   *tuu* 2.
   liutuuagna gerund.
   valiutuu v.t., to prevent, encompass.
liva, centipede : *liva tora*, phosphorescent centipede.   Fl. *liva*.
livo(gna), mouth, beak, point.
   Fl. *livo*, tooth.
livu v.t., to put, dismiss : *hagore
   livu*, to say good-bye to.
   livusagi v.t., to entrust, to
   overfill, be overfull.
   livusagini v.t., to leave, forsake,
   leave behind.
   veilivugi, to give to one another.
lobere, bamboo bass pipe.
lodu, pit.   R. *lovu*.
loga, a pair.   S. *ilo'a*, a fellow wife.

logu, a stream.
longgu, a hollow, depression, valley.   S. *lo'u*, bent ; Fl. *longgu*,
   harbour.
lologa, to roll about, wallow, of
   pig.   V. *loha*.
   loaloga, waterspout.   *viriloga*.
longa, see *i longa, thonga*.   Fl.
   longa.
lopo, to be in a roll, rolled up, to
   reef a sail : *lopo i guema*, a
   measure, from finger-tip to
   elbow-joint.
   loolopo v.t., to fold : *kutu
   loolopo*, intestines.
loso, glossy, shining, of hair or
   feathers.
loulogu(gna), spleen, gall.
lovogata, to cry out, make a loud
   sound ; report of gun, the
   rattle of a lime spatula in a
   gourd.
lua(gna) 1, neck.   U. *lua*.
lua 2, to utter, emit, of sound, to
   vomit.   *lulu* 2.   M. *lulua* ;
   Fl. *lua*.
lualuka, yaws.
lubati v.t., to give, release.   Fl.
   luba.
   lubatiagna gerund.
lufa voc., father.
luhu, thwart of canoe.   S. *lusu*.
lui, torch, lamp (late).   Fl. *lui*.
luka : *na luka i mono*, everything.
luku, to be confined to the house
   through illness ; a cripple.
lulu 1, to leak, melt, to water, of
   eyes : *ke lulu na okogna*, he
   foamed at the mouth.   V.
   lulu.
   valulu v.t., to shed, of blood.
lulu 2, to vomit.   *lulumu* ; *lua* 2.
   lulua v.n., vomit.

lulugua, to choke, of thorns, etc.

luluja, cargo. U. *luda*.

   lujagini v.t., to load cargo.

lulumu, to nauseate, be poison-ous ; nausea : *thehe lulumu*, to die of poisoning. *lulu* 2.

luma(gna), cave. Fl. *vatu luma*.

lumi v.t., to dip into water, cleanse, wash, of feet or clothes. Fl. *lumi*.

   lumiagna gerund.

lumuhi : *gagana lumuhi*, to take a delight in, be concerned about.

lumusa, moss. S. *lumu*.

lupa, to be dropsical ; dropsy. Fl. *lupa* ; U. *pula*.

luti v.t., to forbid, grudge, keep back. S. *lu'i*.

   lutiagna gerund.

luukama, lobster.

luvaolu(gna), a youth, period of youth. *vaolu*. Fl. *luvaolu*.

luvu, to perish, drown, capsize of canoe, become extinct, come to nothing. Fl. *luvu*.

   luvusagini v.t., to die out from a place, of persons.

   valuvu v.t., to destroy.

M

ma 1, adjectival prefix, *manggoru* ; *maliu* ; *malumu* ; *mamaluha*. Melanesia generally. (*mama*).

ma 2, conjunction, and ; the vowel of *ma* shifts in agree-ment with the first vowel of the following word ; viz. *me*, *mi*, *mo*, *mu*. The form *mi* is often preferred when the following vowel is other than *i* : *thevu mi thevu*, part and part ; and *me* is used as a connective when the following vowel is other than *e* ; *me* also denotes ' or '. The vowel of *ma* drops before the pronouns *u*, I, *o*, thou, and before the v.p. *ati*, *iti*, *oti*, *ena*, and before the locative *i*. Fl. *ma*.

maa, to be fearless, of firm mind ; confidence.

maaloa, sky, firmament, heaven. S. *loa*.

maamala, leaning over, sideways.

maamagna, to lust, desire intensely ; lust. *magnahagi*.

maamatha, to be light in weight, easy : *maamatha vaivine*, to be ill developed, not well grown. L., Fl. *mamala*.

mada, to be ripe, of fruit. Fl. *mada*.

madarua, over ripe.

madaki, to be smooth, of plank.

madali, slippery. *dadali*. Fl., S. *madali*.

madoa, to forget.

madotho(gna), right hand, on the right. Fl. *madolo*.

maedu : *kutu maedu*, to stagger, reel. *kutu* 2.

maemate : *vahagi maemate*, plague. Fl. *mate*.

magavu(gna) 1, a day.

magavu 2, a storm.

magi trans. suffix to vb. : *goromagi*. Fl. *magi*.

magohu, insecure, unsafe, as house with rotten posts, axe with cracked handle.

magu adv., presently, wait a while ! *magugua* adv., directly, present-ly, by and by, a little while.

maha, to be deep of sea ; the deep sea. *jagimaha.*

mahavu, stone axe.

maho v.t., to open the mouth by squeezing the cheeks, of person or fish.

mahu, to be replete with food, satisfied. Fl. *mahu* ; U. *masu.*

mai 1, to come ; adv., hither : *kena mai ivei*, whence come they ? *na mai regiugna*, coming to see me ; *na mainggu*, my coming ; *turugugna mai*, from the beginning ; *mai i Pirihadi*, from Pirihadi (here). Fl. *mai.*

maia v.n., coming.

mai 2, trans. suffix to vb. : *pala, palamai.* S. *ma'i.*

majoli, tired.

majora, malice, ill-will, plot, treachery. V. *mazora.*

maku, to be hard, firm, fixed.

mangginggi, to be in uproar, excited, of crowd ; n., tumult.

manggoli, disheartened, dispirited, weary in body or mind, to oversleep. *ma* 1.

manggoru onomatop., to snore. *ma* 1. S. *ngora.*

malaareare, a storm.

malaga : *tango malaga*, to be able ; followed by a gerundive.

malakuni, to beckon.

malehenggo, to bow the head, droop. (*maemalehenggo*).

malesua, adj., faint.

maliolio adj., pleased ; to gain, profit : *na malioliomu*, your profit. *ma* 1.

maliu adj., projecting : *nago maliu*, to project, stick out ; to pass by. *liu.*

maluate, soft, smooth. *malumu.*

malumu adj., level, even, easy, soft. *ma* 1. M. *malumlum.* (*maumalumu*).

malumuagini v.t., to soften, deal gently with, to be easy for.

mama voc., father, sir.

mamanggo, to covet ; covetousness.

mamala, to be cracked.

mamaluha adj., loosed, free, at liberty. *ma* 1 ; U. *luha*, to loose.

mamaluhaga v.n., freedom, liberty.

vamamaluha v.t., to loose, free.

mamara, the paper mulberry.

mamatho, to rest ; n., rest : *togo mamatho*, a resting place. S. *mamalo.*

mami, sweet, agreeable, pleasant, to the taste. L. *mamasia.* Malagasy, *ma-mi.*

famaimami v.t., to flatter.

mana 1, spiritual or magical power, enchantment, power, ability. *tangomana.* Mel. *mana. manangi* v.t., to empower.

mana(gna) 2, equal, like, sufficient. Fl. *mana.*

mane, male, male person : *mane gano, pau ni mane*, adult male ; *mane taulagi*, bridegroom ; *mane kavena*, a watchman ; *na manegna na ruru*, a man of the place ; used to denote sex : *nggari mane*, boy ; *na kau na mane*, bullock. S. *mwane.*

manea, he ; used before personal names : *manea a Kamakajaku*, Kamakajaku. *mane.*

manihihi v.t., to respect, reverence, honour. S. *mani* in *manikulu'e*.

maimanihihiana v.n., an object of reverence.

maimanihihiagna gerund.

manivi adj., thin. *ma* 1. M. *mavinvin*.

manu, bird, a fishing kite : *na manugna na bongi*, a night bird. Mel. *manu*.

maumanu, insect.

manu popo : *thehe manu popo*, to die suddenly.

manga, space, time, air ; to be open, of space ; empty, of village : L., Fl. *manga*.

maamanga, aperture, chink.

mangahagi, to be parched, of ground, to be short of garden food ; n., dearth, summer time.

mangiru, to warm oneself at a fire. Fl. *madiru*.

manguni, a scented shrub.

magnahagi, to regard with favour, choose. *maamagna*.

magnahagini v.t.

magnahaginiagna gerund.

magnivo, hornet. Fl. *manivo*. S. *niho*, tooth.

maolagi, to subside, of waters, to ebb, of tide.

maomamo, to be shy, ashamed.

maomao, to poison by magic, using dried liver of a snake. Fl. *maomao*.

maomaova, to yawn, gape. Fl. *maovo*.

mapongga adj., bruised, of skin ; a bruise.

mara 1, people : *na mara i Higota*, the people of Higota ; *kekeha*

mara, certain people ; used as plural of persons : *mara ke puhi*, the adults ; *mara na tabu*, the saints ; *mara na thaba*, the rulers ; used in address : *mara*, you people ! *tolu mara*, you three, you ! S. *mwala* ; L. *ngwala* ; *Mala, Mara*, the native name of Malaita Island. New Hebrides *mara*, pl. sign.

mara 2, to be discouraged, of mind.

maragata, a wave. Fl. *maragata*, storm.

marai : *na marai*, those persons. *mara* 1.

maraia, they. *mara* 1.

maraira, they : *na maraira*, these people. *mara* 1.

maramagna, the world, the neighbouring islands. L. *maramana*.

marara n., light. Fl. *marara*.

marea, they. *mara* 1.

maria, they. *mara* 1.

maruahe, to sigh. *ahe*.

maruha adj., crushed, broken small. *ma*.

masi, basket.

mata(gna), eye, face, covering, entry. Fl. *mata*.

matagu, to fear, be afraid. Fl. *matagu*. (*maamatagu*).

mamataguana v.n., a fearful thing ; awful, dreadful.

mataguni v.t.

mataguniagna gerund.

matakuni, to wink, wave to, beckon. *mata*. V. *matakuni*.

mateana, planet.

mativi(gna), loins, hips ; to be hollow-bellied : *i mativigna*, on the hip, by one's side.

matoba, landslip.

maturingita, to dream ; a dream. M. *maturu*, to sleep. (*maumaturingita*).

matha(*gna*), bed-mat, bed, sail ; used with *i*, genitive, to denote ' place ' : *matha i lui*, candle-stick ; *matha i vathe*, site of house, ruins ; *matha i lima*, handiwork ; *matha i sono*, a measure, from finger-tip to breast-bone. Fl. *mala*.

mathagai, a champion, might. Fl. *malagai*.

mathagaihagini v.t., to do violence to.

vamathagai v.t., to overpower.

mathangani, new, fresh : *vaivine mathangani*, young girl.

vamathangani v.t., to renew.

mathathe, garden.

mathatho, to feel cold, to have malaria ; cold shivers, malaria. M. *malaso*.

mathothe, the large garfish. S. *mwalole* ; Fl. *malole*.

mathehu, like, as if.

maumavu(*gna*), dust : *maumavu i thepa*, dust of the earth ; *maumavu i tahi*, sea spray.

mause, to be weary, done up.

mauni v.t., to fear. U. *mauni*.

maumauniga adj., fearful, dreadful.

mavara, stony ground.

mavini, to throb. *ma 1*. Arosi *hinihini*, to feel.

mavitu(*gna*), people ; to be general, epidemic : *na mavitu-gna na meleha*, the people of a place. Fl. *mavitu*.

mavo, to heal up, be healed. Fl. *mavo* ; M. *mawo*.

vamavo v.t., to heal.

mavu(*gna*), namesake. Fl. *mavu* ; V. *mavu*.

me, and. *ma 2*.

mee, to be foolish, silly : *kilo meemee*, to be importunate.

vameemee v.t., to make foolish.

meemeenggili, foolish, stupid, silly.

mengga, an edible nut.

mela, red. *metha*. M. *mera*, red sky.

meleha(*gna*) 1, place, land, village.

meleha 2, to be tame, of bird : *na guagua meleha*, a tame cockatoo.

metha, red. *mela*.

meomeo(*gna*), infant, infancy. Fl. *meomeo*.

mi 1, trans. suffix to vb. : *iju*, *ijumi*. S. *mi*.

mi 2, and. *ma 2*.

midoru, a jet, spout, fountain.

mije, cliff, precipice (inland) ; to be precipitous.

mijua, native bee, honey. Fl. *midua* ; S. *ngingidue*.

mike, Jew's harp. R. *mike*.

minggoi, lest ; precedes vb. ; may be preceded by v.p. *e*, or by *nggi*, or *nggi e* : *nggati minggoi thehe*, lest we die ; *koti minggoi veihuhugugi*, see that you do not quarrel among yourselves ; *nggi e minggoi vareogo*, lest thou be destroyed.

mimiraha, to warm oneself in the sun : *ke mimiraha na aoao*, the crow suns itself, the time of day just before sunset.

mimi, urine ; to urinate. Mel. *mimi*, *meme*.

mimi toto, urine.

miniotha, stones used in native oven.

miomilo, to be destitute ; destitution.

vamiomilo v.t., to curse.

miu, suffixed pron. of possession, your.

miuminggu, to smile.

miumisu, to chop, cut, grate.

miumitu(gna), kidney.

moko, hand net, Southern Cross constellation. L. *moke*.

mola, numeral, ten thousand : *na mola*. S. *mola*.

momole, red plaited twine.

mono, to abide, dwell, stay, to be, to have some left over ; n., age, behaviour, abiding, place, country : *na monogna*, his place ; *mono haidu, mono hiliga*, neighbour. S. *mono*. (*moomono*).

monoa v.n., abiding place : *na sakai monoadia*, their own home.

monoi, to abide there.

monongi v.t., to abide in.

monogna v.n., abiding : *na monogna*, to abide.

moro(gna), buttock : *bili sisi moro*, anus.

mosu, south, west. *paka*.

moumolu, island.

mu suffixed pron. of possession, thy.

mua suffixed pron. of possession, thy ; used with *ga 1, ni 2*.

muamuha, cooked, of food : *vanga muamuha*, to eat cooked food.

muamugna, deceit, flattery, cajolery. *mugna*.

muamugnali v.t., to deceive, cajole.

mugua adv., indeed, certainly, really ; follows vb. : *e tutuni mugua*, truly ! Fl. *mugua* ; V. *mu*.

vamugua : *sikei vamugua*, yet once more.

muhu, a beetle. Fl. *muhu*.

mui, to be dumb.

muji, to be ripe, of areca nut when it is red.

muki v.t., to caulk with *tita*, putty nut. Fl. *muki*.

mugna, to be sweet. *muamugna*.

mumuja, dried up, of earth.

mumuka, to itch.

muno, caterpillar. S. *muno*.

muomuno, shell money.

mutimara, likeness.

N

na 1, indefinite article, a ; precedes nouns and gerundives ; *na tinoni*, a man ; *na kulaga*, friendship ; *na hava*, what ? anything ; *na fata*, a thing, the thing, that which ; *na toke*, goodness ; *na vatheheugna*, to kill me ; used with the possessive nouns *ga, ni* : *na ninggua*, mine ; *na gamiu*, for you to eat, your food. Fl. *na*.

na 2, demonstr. pron. ; follows a noun or pers. pron. or verb. ; has emphatic use : *inau na*, as for me ; *igoe na*, you it was ! denotes completion of action : *a Christ keda mai na*, when Christ shall have come. Mel. *na*.

na 3, interrog. particle ; occurs at end of sentence : *ahei na*, who is it ? Fl. *ina*.

na 4, particle added to v.p. *e, ke, keda* to denote 3rd pers. pl. : *ena ahoru*, they said ; *kedana mai*, they will come.

naba, to measure, compare, balance, be equal to, fitting, worthy ; *hagore naba*, to speak in parables ; *ke nabamu*, worthy of you ; *ko nabagna a hanu*, you are like so-and-so ; *nanaba sale*, to compose a song ; a song maker.

nanaba, a measure, requital : *bali nanaba*.

vananaba v.t., to requite, render dues.

varinanaba, to be co-equal.

nadi, flint. U. *ngadi*.

nae(gna), leg, foot : *thehe nae*, paralysis, withered leg.

nago, before, in front, first ; the pronouns of possession may be suffixed : *talu nago*, to be proud, to magnify oneself ; *ke nago*, first ; *na nago ma na legu vahui*, the first and the last ; *nago ulu*, headlong ; *nagodia*, before them ; *keda nagogna*, he shall go before him. Fl. *nago* ; M. *nagoi*.

nagoi v.t., to precede, go before.

nagoviagna gerund., before, go before.

nago maliu, to project, protrude, stick out ; the second finger. *maliu*.

nahiga, sand.

nahu, bowl, vegetable mash made in bowl by stone-boiling.

namu exclam. of sorrow, alas !

nana, to tear, break, of net.

nanasa, to be quiet, at peace, safe, to be all in order, right.

vananasa v.t., to set to rights, put right.

nao exclam. of doubt, ' is it so ' ?

nata, level ground, a plain ; to be level. Fl. *nanata*.

nau pers. pron., I ; not in general use. *inau*.

neere, to close the eyes in sleep, to sleep ; n., sleep : *neere thoti*, to sleep soundly.

nere, to be insecure, unsafe.

ni 1, prepositional verb ; precedes a vb., and the pronouns of the object are suffixed ; (1) used as prep. with meanings ' therewith, with, by, to, for ' : *me ke nira havugagi*, and sacrificed therewith ; *me ke nira hage kori hugu*, and there is an entering for them into the harbour ; *nia udu*, to go along with ; *kena nia lealeaa na tootonggo*, they rejoiced with joy ; (2) used as transitive verb meaning ' do, do to ' : (*e*) *hava nia*, how ? why ? *o hava nia eeri*, what are you doing here ? (3) used preceding certain intransitive verbs, the pronouns of the object being added : *ke nia tuhu na limana*, he stretched out his hand ; *nia bati*, to refrain from it. *nia*. Fl., R., *ni*.

ni 2, possessive noun ; the pronouns of possession are always added : *ninggua*, my, *nimua*, thy, *nigna*, his, *nida*, *nimami*, *nimiu*, *nidia* ; used of general relation ; the articles *na, sa* may precede : *na nimiu na vike*, your people ; *na nigna ahai*, whose ? *ninggua na kana*, my enemy ; *matagu ninggua*, I was afraid ; *tangihia ninggua na pohe*, I want some cloth ; used following a verb to denote ' for my part ', etc. : *boi ninggua*, I am unwilling. Fl. *ni*.

ni 3, genitive ; used only in certain phrases : *puku ni mana*, the source of power ; *pau ni mane*, an elder ; *pau ni taviti*, to continue going, keep on going. S., Fl., *ni*.

ni 4, trans. suffix to vb. : *matagu, mataguni*. S. *ni*.

ni 5, noun suffix, used with relationship terms ; *tama-pajani*, cross-cousins ; *tama-tubuni*, mother's brother and sister's son. Fl. *ni*.

ni 6, demonstr. pron., component part of *eni* ; *ngeni*. U. *ni*.

nia instrumental preposition, thereby, therewith, by means of, withal ; precedes the verb or phrase with which it is used : *ke nia poko na pohe*, he is clad with clothes ; *ke nia thabuhia na isi*, he killed him with a sword. *ni* 1. Fl. *nia*.

niagna prep., with, of accompaniment, or instrumental.

nida, to move about, oscillate.

nige exclam. of address, calls attention : you ! I say ! Fl. *gee*.

nigotha, to wipe dry.

ningge, a fork.

niu, coconut and tree : *niu tupa*, a ripe coconut. Sol. Is. *niu*.

niubu, damp.

niuri, brushwood.

nohi, boundary ; used only in the form *nohigna*, 3rd pers. sing.

noinoi, to groan ; a groan.

nono v.t., to wrap food in leaves ready for cooking.

nugu 1 : *hagore nugu*, to speak privately to a person.

nugu 2, to emerge, come out into the open. Fl. *nugu* ; L. *nuu*, reef.

nuguvotu, the point of the reef.

nuilagi, to enable, empower ; used of spiritual power.

nuilagini v.t.

Ng

The sound of *ng* is that of *ng* in English ' sing '.

ngae, to be weary, to weary anyone.

ngaengare, gentle, light, of wind or waves.

ngaengate, to be angry, to rage ; n., anger, rage.

ngagi trans. suffix to vb. : *jata, jatangagi* ; *butungagi*.

ngaja, to rub between the hands, to spin a top, rubbing it between the hands. Fl. *gada*. (*ngaangaja*).

ngali, canarium almond. Sol. Is. *ngali*.

ngaingali, scented leaves.

ngangata 1 : *vele ngangata*, to upbraid. L. *ngata*.

ngangata 2, to suck, chew for juice, as sugar cane, to suck, of infants. Fl. *ngatangata*.

ngapo, turtle-shell.

ngara, to rail, shout at, scold, threaten : *vele ngangara*, to rail at ; *ngangara*, to cry aloud ; a shout. S. *ngara*, to weep.

ngara nguungutu, to hesitate, linger, loiter.

ngasi, to be hard, firm, fixed, strong. Fl. *ngasi*.

vangasi v.t., to harden, make firm.

ngehe, pandanus umbrella.

ngele v.t., to blame, find fault with : *ngele saropagini*, to sneer at, speak contemptuously of. Fl. *ngele*.

fangeengele v.t., to despise.

ngelengele, to commit adultery ; adultery. Fl. *ngele*.

ngeni demonstr. pron., that ; there ; follows a noun.

i ngengeni, there.

ngengere, famine. Fl. *ngengere*.

ngerepe, tobacco.

ngeso, a wound.

fangeso v.t., to wound.

ngi trans. suffix to vb. : *buta*, *butangi*. S. *ngi*.

ngiengigne, to tingle.

ngigi verbal, suffix : *veivulangigi*.

ngiha, how many ! when ? the v.p. *e* may precede : *gathi ngiha*, too few. *i ngiha*. U. *nita*.

ngihagi, when ? how many ? how much ? how long ?

ngiingili, to shout, cry aloud : *ngiingili na sale*, to sing a song. Fl. *ngingili*.

ngigno v.t., to mix, stir, stir up, agitate. (*ngiongigno*).

ngiu, to waggle, move.

ngo, a lizard.

ngoengoe(gna), jaw, chin.   V. *ngongoe*.

ngoi, shoulder bag.

ngoingovi v.t., to flatter.

ngongone, yellow, orange in colour.

ngou, opossum.

nguanguao, old word for ' ship '. *tapalao*.

ngungiti, to pulsate, beat, throb.

ngunguju(gna), image, likeness. Ed. *ngungunguju*.

ngutu 1, to be blunt, hard, of disposition or mind. Fl. *ngutu*.

vangutu v.t., to harden, strengthen.

ngutu 2, to be in labour, of women.

nguunguru onomatop., to roar, of animal.

nguunguu onomatop., to murmur, whisper, speak low. (*nguunguunguu*).

Gn

The sound of *gn* is that of *ni* in English ' onion '. The *gn* is a change from *n*.

gna 1, ligative article ; denotes ' the belonging to ' ; used of both persons and things, the locative *i* being added of places : *na pen gna i velepuhi*, the pen of the teacher ; *a Mary gna i Magdala*, Mary of Magdala. Fl. *na* 2 ; IN. *na*.

gna 2, suffixed pron. of possession, 3rd pers. sing., his, her's, its ; added to nouns, or to nouns used as prepositions. Fl. *na*.

gna 3, verbal noun suffix : *na kasagna*, completion, to com-

plete ; forms compound noun :
na idumi kasa gamugna, your
whole number ; *na sokara
pungusigamugna,* opposing
you, to oppose you ; has
gerundival force ; a pro-
nominal object may be
inserted in the compound : *na
reiregiugna,* the seeing of me,
to see me ; *na vatokeragna,*
the blessing of them, to bless
them ; used following *dia,*
pron. of possession, 3rd pers.
pl., when *dia* follows *ra,*
a gerundival particle : *na
fateradiagna,* to judge them ;
an object may follow the
compound verb : *na palikuti-
radiagna na komi puhi,* the
keeping of, to keep, the laws.
agna.

gna 4, noun suffix, added to
cardinal numbers to make
ordinals.

gnabo, to persist, be busy.
(*gnaognabo*).

gnaegnale, green, of grass.

gnaegnave, sparingly, idly, carelessly, follows verb : *tangoli
gnaegnave,* to take only a few ;
anggutu gnaegnave, to do a
little work only.

gnago 1, to wither, be withered ;
a withered tree.

gnago 2, cicada.

gnagu(gna), a few, part, remnant :
na gnagu i uvi, a few yams.

gnagugnege, ill-tied, disorderly,
carelessly, higgledy-piggledy,
disturbed, confused, in mind.

gnagura, clean, pure.
vagnagura v.t., to cleanse,
purify.

gnanggo, to be tired, faint, weary.
gnanggogna v.n.

gnami v.t., to nibble, bite, taste :
gnami vidogna, to taste a
piece. M. *nam* ; Fl. *nami.*

gnamiagna gerund.

gnamu, mosquito. M. *namu.*

gnagnara, to dry up, of flood
waters.

gnao 1, to abate, subside, of
waters.
gnaoragi, to subside, of waters.
vagnao v.t., to cause to dry up.

gnao(gna) 2, penis.

gnaognabo, to loiter, delay, be
slow.

gnaognato, to shake.

gnapi v.t., to bite, taste. Fl. *napi.*
gnagnapi v.t., to lick.

gnarutu, to be corrupt ; corrup-
tion.

gnaumu, to be green, of grass.

gneku(gna), bird's nest. *gniku.*

gneognebo, to stir, be rough, of sea.

gnegnepa, mud, pitch. M. *lepa* ;
Fl. *nenepa.*

gniigniti, to bite. M. *ngit.*

gniku(gna), bird's nest. *gneku.*
M. *nigiu.*

gnilau v.t., to adorn ; bodily
ornaments. Fl. *nilau* ; S.
launi.
gnilauagna gerund.

gnobe, vegetable pudding.

gnoignoi, gnat. Fl. *noinoi.*

gnolu, a blot, stain.

gnognoro, fornication.

gnoro, a wave, breaker, surf ; to
be rough, of sea.

gnou v.t., to bite, taste.

gnovo, to shake, of spear.
gnovoti v.t., to parry a blow,
ward off a spear.

gnubu, to be wet.

vagnubu v.t., to wet, to water a plant.

gnugu, nose ornament.

gnuignuligagna, budding.

gnujuri v.t., to rub with the hand. *ujuri*.

gnuri, brushwood, green bushes.

gnuria adj., set on fire.

gnuru onomatop., to snore.   S. *ngora*.

O

o, pers. pron., thou ; combines with v.p. *ke* in the form *ko*. Fl. *o*.

oba, rope.

obo, to flood, be flooded ; flood tide : *na jata i obo*, top of the tide ; *na paa i obo*, low tide ; *ke siri na obo*, tide rising. Fl. *obo*.

obohagini v.t., to water a plant. *oboti* v.t., to flood.

odu, palolo viridis. Fl. *odu*.

ofa, to be deserted, of uninhabited house.

ofi v.t., to sit on eggs, hatch.

oga(gna), root. Fl. *oga*.

oha(gna) 1, sound, noise, voice.

ohavi v.t., to increase, of voice.

oha 2, to scatter.

oho(gna), food for a journey. Fl. *oho*.

ohu, to be overgrown, of village site ; a thicket. Fl. *ohu*.

oiobili, to be fat.

oka, war, enemy ; *ganggua na thevu ni oka*, my enemy.

veiokagi, *veiokaokagi*, to be at war with one another.

oko(gna), spittle.

olaola, to peer, gaze about.

oleo, to be dumb.

oli, to change. Fl., S. *oli*.

olihi v.t., to exchange : *olihigna*, in place of it.

vaoli v.t., to exchange ; in turn.

veiolihigi, to exchange.

olo, to bend, stoop : *olo horu*.

oloi, freshwater eel.

oluolu, to be greedy, gluttonous.

oluboli, id.

ono numeral, six. S. *ono*.

onogna, sixth.

onoono, six apiece.

vaonogna, six times.

onohu, a beetle.

onga, lightning.

ongavi v.t., to shine, flash of lightning.

oo, to make a noise.

oogo, to be bent, bowed, to stoop, be downcast, of face.

oogoro, id.

ooho v.t., to take, carry on shoulder ; a weight, burden : *na bali ooho*, a yoke.

oohoagna gerund.

oohonga v.n.

oopo v.t., to wear, put on, of clothes.

oopoagna gerund.

vaoopo v.t., to clothe.

ooro, swamp, mud.

ore v.t., to rebuke.

oriori, to tow alongside.

oro pronominal verbal particle, we two (incl.), you two.

orooro, plummet ; *soni orooro*, to take soundings.

oti pronominal verbal particle, you.

otolu pronominal verbal particle, you three, they three.

otooto(gna), branch. Fl. *oto.*

otho, to swim. S., Fl. *olo.*

ouou onomatop., to cough.

ovi exclam., oh ! hey ! come now !

P

paa, to be quenched, extinguished, of torch : *ifu paa*, to blow out, of a light ; *ke paa na kalai*, it is low tide ; *paa horu*, to calm down, of sea.

paapanga, to pant, be tired.

pada v.t., to hit, strike, meet, find, happen, happen to, succeed ; *hara pada*, to encounter, come across ; *pada rongo*, to be rich.

padagna v.n.

veipadagi to encounter, meet, of two people.

padagi(gna), a sanctuary. Fl. *padagi.*

pafu : *thehe pafu*, to die a natural death, not through magic ; *na vahagi pafu*, fever.

pagana, fruitless, in vain : *hai pagana*, to lack ; *mena pagana*, and they did it in vain.

pahala, to cleave, be cloven.

pahe v.t., to cut, cut off : *pahe vaugithatha*, to circumcise (late). Fl. *pahe*. (*paepahe*).

paheagna gerund.

papahe, a knife.

paike, an opossum.

paipaki, an ornamented paddle.

paipaligi, to be ignorant, stupid.

paingoti, to take root, make firm.

paipaliku, to blink.

paja(gna), cross-cousin.

tamapajani, cross-cousins.

paji v.t., to drive, chase, hunt : *paji au*, to drive out.

pajiagna gerund.

papaji v.t., to persecute ; n., hunting, persecution.

pachangguanggura, to foam, froth. *ngguanggura.*

paka adv., over there, south, west : *thevu pakagna*, on the far side.

paki 1, red shell-money ; 2, to stain.

paipaki, coloured a brilliant red.

pakoto(gna), stopper of leaves, cork for bamboo water-carrier.

pangga, herd ; specific numeral, ten, of pigs. Fl. *pangga.*

panggala : *piri panggala*, sling for slinging stones. *pupuru panggala.*

pangge, to begin ; a beginning : *pangge hagore*, to begin to speak ; *kena eu pangge ifu*, they began to play the pipes.

panggehi v.t., to turn partly over, lift up one side.

panggu v.t., to join, graft ; a joint. Fl. *panggu*. (*paupanggu*). *pangguagna* gerund.

panggusu(gna), a generation : *na panggusu ma na panggusu*, throughout all generations.

pala v.t., to embrace, carry in the arms. S. *'apala*. (*paapala*).

palamai v.t. : *palamai vano*, to hand over a child into another person's arms.

pala olihi v.t., to exchange, of money, etc.

palabatu, example, pattern ; to set an example, lead off. *batu.*

palaku v.t., to strike, blast, of lightning or wind.

palakue, to carry on a pole, of two men.

palala, ridge, crest, top, of hill, head ; to be bald : *palala i suasupa*, crest of hill.

paligi v.t., to conceal.

palikuti v.t., to keep, tend, guard. Fl. *kuti*, give food to.

palikutiagna gerund.

paluha(gna), error, mistake.

pama v.t., to sew two things together.

pamu v.t., to press, compress.

pango v.t., to muzzle.

pao, cage for decoy fish, cupboard for vegetables. S. *pao*.

papa v.t., to carry pick-a-back. S. *haha* ; R. *papa*.

papari, to take a vow, to fast till the completion of a vow.

papaumu : *puni papaumu*, pitch dark.

papauro, quicksands : *kolo papauro*, the lake with quicksands guarding the entrance to Tuhilagi.

para v.t., to afflict, to burn, scorch, of sun. Fl. *para*.

paapara v.t., to injure, hurt, afflict, to suffer, to warm up food ; n., affliction, anguish.

paragna v.n., affliction, anguish.

parafu, ashes. *pidarafu*.

paraka, bag, basket.

parako, white cloud. Fl. *parako*.

parangaha, to be irritating, unpleasant to the taste, uncomfortable, as bed. *para*.

paritina, dry land, shore. *tina*. Fl. *pari*, land.

paru v.t., to betroth : *taulagi paru*.

pasa, to be empty.

pataka, to hang round the neck ; necklace. Fl. *papataka*. (*paapataka*).

patu 1, to be hard, firm, taut : *patu nggama*, to be hard as *nggama*. Fl. *patu*.

patu 2 : *hotagi patumiu*, in your midst ; *hinaota patu*, midday. Fl. *patu*.

pau 1, indigo. Fl. *pau*.

pau 2, head ; to continue, go straight on : *pau ni mane*, an elder ; *pau ni taviti*, to go straight on, an uninterrupted going. U. *qau*.

paupaku, to endure, be patient. *gathapaku*. Fl. *paku*, thick.

pakua adj , enduring, long suffering.

pava, plank. V. *pava*.

peda, a grain, unit, disk of shell money. Fl. *peda*.

pedo, amiss : *hagore pedo*, to speak wide of the mark ; *gagana pedo*, to think amiss. (*peopedo*).

pejuragi, to stumble, limp.

vapejuragi v.t., to cause to stumble.

peko, large canoe, with raised stem and stern. Fl. *peko*.

penggo, to deceive ; deceit. V., Fl. *penggo*. (*peopenggo*).

penggu, fish hook of pearl shell.

pelo 1, to cross over.

pelongi v.t.

pelo 2, hill.

penutu, coconut husk, brush of same. Fl. *penutu* ; V. *penggu*.

peo v.t., to fence, a fence : *hagore peo*, to make one's defence in speech. Fl. *peo*.

peopeo, to shade, hide, shelter ; a shade, shelter.

peoti v.t., to fence, hide from view.

vapeo v.t., to guard.

pepepe, to stammer.

peperiki, to be startled, to jump when startled.

vapeperiki v.t., to startle, cause amazement to.

pepetei v.t., to touch, handle, feel.

pero v.t., to betray. S. *pwelo*. (*peopero*).

peroagna gerund.

peso, to be empty, dry, of woman's breast : *peso susuu*, dry breast, the last child.

vapeso v.t., to cause to dry up.

petekuna, to strain, as in lifting a weight. *kuna*.

pidaravu, ashes. *parafu*. Fl. *ravu*.

pidi, to spring, rebound : *pidi hadi*, to bounce, spring up, of a trap or branch released. Fl. *pidi*.

pidilagi(ni) v.t., to make an offering to a ghost by way of propitiation, burning food or laying it on a grave : *na bali pidilagi*, a propitiation.

piditao, to be brimful. *tao*.

pido v.t., to break up small, of firewood : *piopido i gai*, sticks.

pijiri v.t., to plait with three or four strands. Fl. *pidiri*.

pijiriagna gerund.

pikihu(gna), stump, stubble.

piko v.t., to dislocate, be dislocated.

pingge v.t., to turn, twist.

pinggu specific numeral, ten, of coconuts : *sikei na pinggu*, ten coconuts. *Fl. pinggu*.

pila, to be soft, flexible, ripe. S. *pile*.

pilau, to deceive.

piapilau, to lie : *tango piapilau*, to deal deceitfully.

pili v.t., to practise, attempt, try, prove, to feint when attacking an enemy. (*piipili*).

piliagna gerund.

piliu, to return, turn round ; adv., again, back ; follows vb. *liu*.

pilu v.t., to fence, surround, put in enclosure, of pig ; an enclosure for a pig or a tree. Fl. *pilu* ; V. *pipilu*.

pilungi v.t., to turn round, reverse, subvert.

pinarasa, glowing firebrands ; to burn like a firebrand.

pinatoti, to stay at home, settle down.

piniru, to encamp ; a camp : *talu piniru*, to make a camp.

piniti, to tie up a canoe, to anchor. Fl. *piniti*.

pinu, a hollow.

pipiala, tobacco pipe ; to smoke tobacco. Fl. *pipiala*.

pipiringgo, a trifle, elemental thing : *na fata pipiringgo*.

pipiutu, rainbow.

piri 1, belt, rope : *piri voovogo*, waist-belt.

piri 2, v.t., to stone with stones. M. *vivir* ; Fl. *pirikagini*.

piriagna gerund.

piricho, summit, top, of tree or mountain, sky line, horizon.

piriloho, to dance : a dance.

piru, rope, line : *soni piru*, night fishing with line.   M. *vir* ; Fl. *piru*.

piruki v.t., to twist, wrench, screw, plait.

pisangi v.t., to add.

pisari to slap with the hand, beat against, as flood or surf, to slap an offering placed on a grave. Fl. *pisa*.

pisi v.t., to gird, bind, wrap up food for cooking : *pisi kilili*, to throng, crowd round : *pohe piipisia*, a skirt.   M. *vivis* ; Fl. *pisi*.

pisiagna gerund.

pisupaa adv., utterly, altogether, completely, finished, come to naught ; follows a vb.   Fl. *pisu*, to pass away ; V. *piju*.

piti, a snare, noose : *talu piti*, to be ensnared. Fl. *piti*.

piipiti v.t., to snare.

piti konggu, to tow behind, to lead with a rope. *piti*.

pitu v.t., to await, wait, expect : *mono pitu*. Fl. *pitu*.

pituagna gerund.

veipitupitugi, to wait for one another.

piupidu, to gird.

poapoga, house posts on sides, side of canoe.

poda, to hatch. *ofi*.

podilo, with a bang, at one swoop.

poepote i nae, calf of leg.

pogo, to incline the body, stoop, bow : *pogo horu*. Fl. *pogo*.

poguru 1, roof of house.

poguru 2, the back ; to be humpbacked.

poha, to burst, discharge, of boil,

to crack, be cracked, to break, of day or surf, crack, of rifle.

poapoha, crack, opening, cleft : *poapoha i livo*, lips.

poapoha i thabota, day-break.

pohali v.t. : *huru pohali*, to press and burst.

pohe, bark cloth, cloth : *pohe piipisi*, skirt, clothing.   Fl. *pohaga*.

poholo, coconut and taro mash ; to make the mash.

poipodilo, to burn.

poipokite, to be rough, with inequalities, of road, undressed timber, etc.

pojaga, foul, discoloured, of water. *vapojaga* v.t., to defile.

poji v.t., to wring, squeeze, twist. Fl. *posi*, to tie. (*popoji*).

pocho, a sponge.

poko(gna), clothes : *ni poko*, to put on clothes ; *pohe poko*, coat ; *ke nia poko na pohe*, he wore clothes.

vapokoagna gerund.

pokusu, hill.

poli, snake. Fl. *poli*.

polo, to hide, be hidden : *talu polo*, to hide : *tango poopolo*, to act the hypocrite. Fl. *polo*.

poloa adj., secretly.

poloagna gerund.

polohagini v.t., to conceal, hide from.

pona, many, much.

pono, to be closed up, stuffed up : *rodo pono*, darkness ; *pono hehe*, heedless, careless.   S. *pono*.

ponoi v. t., to work at, be occupied with.

ponoti v.t., to close, mend, muzzle with the hand.

ponotiagna gerund.

poopono, pooponoti, a patch.

pongo, to be worried by a thing, distressed, occupied mentally with.

poopongo, to covet.

pognoi v.t., to grasp, squeeze, defraud. Fl. *pongo.*

pognu, to disappear from sight. Fl. *ponu.*

pooporo, reeds.

popo 1, above, top : *popogna,* its top, on it, above, after ; *i popogna suasupa,* on the top of the hill ; *vula i popo,* next month. Fl. *kokou.*

popo 2, wooden bowl. Fl. *popo.*

popone, breadfruit tree.

popoo, to sting and blister, of nettle tree.

popotoio, fat.

popu, to be full. Fl. *popu.*

pora, debt ; to discharge a debt, repay.

poro, pineapple.

poroulu, to become tributary to. *ulu.*

poru, to be slow, loiter, delay, be a long time, be dull of hearing. (*pouporu*).

posilego, a measure, finger's length, fork of thumb to top of first finger.

posomogo, name of a marriage clan. *thogokama ; vihuvunagi.*

potajimei, waterfall.

pote, to be full-grown. V. *pote.*

poto, a folk-lore tale : *tuguni poto.*

potu, to fly, of arrow.

potua adj., *rage potua,* to run swiftly.

pothoho v.t., to cross over.

pouporu, sea louse.

puala adv., very, much ; follows vb.

puepurere, split in two, asunder.

pueti v.t., to cause to shine, of eyes.

pugu, to cook on embers, burn, to heat water, boil : *ai bali pugu,* firewood ; *pugu juru,* to burn up. Fl. *pugu.*

puguli v.t., to stew in a bamboo, boil water in a kettle.

puguliagna gerund.

puhi(gna), custom, usage : *tinoni puhi,* an adult.

vapuhi v.t., to instruct.

pui, to be deaf ; deaf mute. Fl. *pui.*

fapuipui kuli, to be hard of hearing.

puingi v.t., to press, oppress. (*puipuingi*).

puingiagna gerund.

puipui, native oven ; to cook in native oven.

puipuki, to drop, of liquid ; a drop.

puipuli 1, to pull out facial hair by depilation, scissors (modern).

puipuli 2, the bivalve shell used for depilation.

puju, to melt, dissolve.

pucha, to spring up, of plants.

puchaoko, to be contrary, factious,

puku 1, a swelling from a blow, lump, knot, tumour. Fl. *varipuku,* knot. (*puupuku*).

puku 2, n., real, complete : *na puku ni tinoni,* a true man ; *na puku ni tutuni,* the very truth ; *na puku ni sisi,* wholly red ; *puku ni mana*, almighty. Fl. *puku*.

puku(gna) 3, of one's own accord, one's own ; to possess : *ku pukugna na meleha*, I own the place ; *na pukunggu*, my very own ; *na ninggua na pukunggu*, of my own accord. *puku* 2.

puloku(gna), elbow.

puloso, broken, of reed.

pululu, lost, unaccounted for : *thehe pululu*, to die from an unknown cause.

pulungagi, to sink, subside.

puni, dark cloud, darkness : *rodo puni*, darkness ; *puni horu*, dark ; *ke puni doka*, pitch dark. Fl. *pui* ; *pungi*.

vapuni v.t., to darken.

punui, a faggot.

pungusi v.t., to cover, conceal ; used as prep., over, against, in opposition to. Fl. *pungusi*.

pungusiagna gerund : *na sokara pungusiagna*, to oppose.

pugnoku v.t., to clasp, clinch.

pupuru panggala, a sling for slinging stones ; to sling stones. *panggala*. V., Ed., Fl. id.

pupuruma, piece, morsel.

pura, white : *mane pura*, a white man; *hangga pura*, palish. Fl. *pura*.

puapura, undyed, of bark cloth.

pure, women's string skirt.

purisi : *thabu purisi*, to cut off.

purungongojo v.t., to smash, pulverize.

purusagi, to overflow.

pusi v.t., to smite, beat, hit, slap. Fl. *pusi* ; M. *vus*.

puipusi v.t., to thump, hit with stick, thrash.

pusiagna gerund.

puupuku i thepa, footstool. *puku* 1.

puu, edible fungus growing on trees. V. *puu*.

puupulu, banyan.

R

ra 1, suffixed pron. of the object, 3rd pers. pl., used of persons and things. U. *ra*.

ra 2, infixed gerundival particle, added to trans. verb, with *dia* following, and gerundive ending *gna* : *na ijumiradiagna*, the counting of, to count, them. *a* 8. S. *la*.

raba, to climb.

rabaha(gna), ulcer : *rarabaha*, to be ulcerous ; ulcerous person, leper (late).

rabo, to scatter, throw broadcast ; used with *ni* 1. Fl. *rabo*.

rakokagini v.t., to scatter broadcast.

rade, large size porpoise tooth, used as money. Fl. *rade*.

rae, to be excessive : *ena hava rae kutu*, how great was their fall !

rage, to run ; *rage legu*, to requite, revenge, inquire about ; vengeance. Fl. *rage*.

ragevi v.t., to run to.

veiragevigi, to spend ; gain, profit.

ragi verbal suffix : *gnaoragi*.

rago, to be prostrate, to prostrate oneself.

ragomu, a crab.

ragova, fat, adipose matter. U. *rakuha*.

raha, to nauseate.

rahe, to pine away, of a person, to waste, wither, of body.

rai, a dwarf.

raii, to borrow.

rangga(gna), chest, breast, bosom. Fl. *rangga*.

ranggi, to dance up and down ; a dance.

rano, to flood ; a flood. Malagasy *rano*, water.

ranga hehe, to be undecided.

rangana, ladder.

rangi, to shine, of sun. V. *rangi* ; U. *raangi*.

rarangi, heat.

rango, to wither, of leaves, yam vines. S. *rango*.

raorao, to fish with a net.

rapo, to be roofed in, of house ; to be plaited, of club handle.

rapobete, to be withered, of limb, to tie a rafter to ridge pole, *bete*. Fl. *rapobete*.

rarago, to take shelter from wind or rain.

raorago, to trust.

raragogna v.n., shelter.

raraha v.t., to shine, enlighten, to be clean, clear ; a bright light.

dani raraha, daybreak. U. *rara*.

vararaha v.t., to make clean or clear.

rarahi v.t., to carve, chisel.

rarai, to awake, to waken. Fl. *rai* ; Arosi *rarai*.

vararai v.t.

raraja, to crack an almond in one blow ; adv., in a flash.

rarange, to warm oneself at a fire.

rarovi v.t., to pity. M. *magarosa* ; Fl. *arovi*.

raorarovi, pitiable.

raroviagna gerund.

veirarovi, mutual sympathy, mutual suffering.

rata, a grove or plantation of nut trees.

ra-u 1, cat's cradle, the string game.

rau 2, to be desolate, to be a stranger : *mono rau*.

rava, to endure, suffer uncomplainingly ; used with *ni* 1.

ravagna gerund.

ravita, to lean, trust, rely : *ravita atu* ; used with *ni* 1.

regi v.t., to see : *regia*, look ! behold ! *regi pada, regi padagna*, to find, come across ; *talu regi*, to see ; *regi thehe*, a portent, marvel ; used as prep. of motion towards. *rei*. Fl. *rigi*. (*reiregi*).

regiagna gerund.

veiregi, veiregigi, veireiregigi, to see one another, look at one another.

rei, to look : *rei vano*, to look beyond ; *kati reireida*, let us look. Fl. *rei*.

fareirei : *na bali fareirei*, a thing for seeing, spectacle.

reihoru, to see upside down, name of a fish that swims upside down.

reirei(gna), appearance, look.

reirovi, eyeglasses.

reka, cramp.

renggohi v.t., to smash, break a tree, of lightning.

reo v.t., to destroy; a ruin, destruction.

reogna, vareonga, v.n., destruction.

vareo v.t., to destroy, consume.

reokejo, to be violent; violence : *reoreokejo,* violent behaviour.

reoreo, a shield.

rere aba, wide, spacious. *aba.*

rerengge, a twig.

resu v.t., to tear, rend.

resuagna gerund.

resugna v.n.

rete, to crash, of thunder; thunder.

ri 1, demonstrative; has explanatory use, softens speech; follows a pron. or vb. : *inau ri,* it is I. *ari, eri* ; Mala *ri.*

ri 2, trans. suffix to vb. : *tapo, tapori.* U. *ri.*

ria, a fishing net.

ribo v.t., to splash, to churn up, of water.

rihu, to fight, be at war; a fight.

veiriurihugi, to fight one another, be at war.

rikiraka, to be dispersed, scattered, as matches out of a box.

ririana, to be ready.

ririhi, to comb out fibre, to be digitated, of leaf.

ririti, to be greedy.

riso v.t., to draw, drag, write.

rioriso(gna), writing, book.

risoa passive, written.

risoagna gerund.

riu, to move position, change place of, move a house : *mono (talu) riuriu,* to wander about, be on the move. Fl., R., *riu.*

riuriugabi, the black and white fantail. *riu.* S. *riuriukape.*

ro, numeral, two; denotes dual number : *ro limadia na vaivine,* the hands of the two women; *irotadia,* with the two of them; *ro vavinegna,* his two sisters; *ro iira na vaivine,* the two women; *na ro matamiu,* the eyes of you two; used as a noun : *na romiu,* belonging to, of, you two; *na rodia,* their property. *rua.* S. *ro.*

roa 1, a frog.

roa 2 : *tao i roa,* bridge of the nose.

roai(gna), the gums.

rodo, night; used only in *rodo pono,* pitch dark, *rodo puni,* darkness. S. *rodo.*

rofe, a fishing rod.

rofo, hunger; to be hungry : *na rofomu,* you are hungry.

rogami, we two (excl.). *ro.*

rogamu, you two. *ro.*

rogita, we two (incl.). *ro.*

roira, they two : *roira koro soesole,* they two were naked. *ro.*

roku, mourning garments of barkcloth; to mourn. Fl. *roku.*

romaraira, romarea, they two. *ro.*

romo, darkness.

ronu v.t., to wait for, expect. R. *ronu.*

rouronuagna gerund.

rongo(gna), red shell-money, generic term for shell-money : *soni rongo,* to subscribe money. Fl. *rongo.*

rongoraga, fame, glory; to be famous. *rongovi.*

roorongo, to hear, receive a report ; news, tidings. *rongovi*. Mel. *rongo*.

rongovi v.t., to hear.
rongoviagna gerund.
roorongogna v.n., hearing.
varongo v.t., to hear, listen to, obey : *gagana vaovarongo*, to meditate : *mara na vaovarongo*, the disciples.

rorojo, to wail, of women.

rosa, to be scattered, dispersed, by floods or enemies.
rosavi v.t., to carry away, of flood, scatter, overwhelm.

rote v.t., to pour out, pour away, pull down, of fence : *rote horu*, to bear abundantly, of nut tree. Fl. *rote*.
rotea passive, fallen down, of stone fence, fallen off, poured out.
roteagna gerund.

rua, numeral two : *(e)ruarua*, two at a time, two apiece. Mel. *rua*.
ruagna, varuagna, second.
varuai, twice, second time : *ke varuai kilogna*, called him a second time.

ruaruva, a charm, amulet, divination.
ruvati v.t., to divine.
ruvatiagna gerund, divination.

ruavatu, bamboo water-carrier, with two or more joints. *rua*.

rubau, to smear with clay, paint.

rugi, to slip, slide.

rugu, to duck the head : *rugu au*, to go out of a house ; *hagore rugu*, to speak privately. S. *ru'u* ; V. *ruju* ; Fl. *rugu*.
ruguvi v.t., to travel through.
varugu v.t., to put under, insert.

ruja v.t., to rub, wash, erase.

rujugi v.t., to strip off, remove, of clothing.

runggu, to flower, produce fruit ; a flower.

runggusi, to be busy, work hard ; business : *runggusi pedo*, to meddle, be a busybody ; *runggusigna*, he is busy.
varunggusi v.t., to busy oneself with.

rumu, dugong. R. *rumu*.

rura, to be phosphorescent.

ruru, a village ; v.t., to build a village. S. *ruru*, to gather together.

rurugu, a bivalve, unio.

ruubala, tumult, confusion, uproar, clamour.

S

sa 1, article, one, the, a, any ; used with *teo*, negative : *sa hanu*, so-and-so, any person, some one ; *sa nigna fata*, his things ; *sa lage*, ten ; *e teo sa hanu*, there is no one ; *e teo sa fata*, there is nothing. *MIL*. pp. 63 (6), 544, *sa*.

sa 2, to forbid, a taboo mark forbidding entrance to a place or taking the thing marked. V. *vaja*, oath.

sa 3, dehortative ; not used of plural : *o sa sigo au*, don't look out ! used also as strong negative : *o sa dorovia*, you shall not see him. *sa* 2 ; *sagoi*.

sa 4, adjectival suffix : *lumusa*. M. *sa*.

saasama, to be in need, needy.

saasangara, to lament, cry aloud, howl. *ngara*.

saasangavi v.t., to tear, rend.

saba 1 : *lau saba*, careless, heedless ; *hai lau sasaba*, to act heedlessly towards.

saba 2, to bump, graze, come in contact with, meet and pass. *veisasabagi*, to meet one another.

sabiri v.t., to barter, buy, market. Fl. *sabiri*. (*saisabiri*).

sabiriagna gerund.

sadi, barren.

saesangge, basket.

sagaro(gna), fruit on the tree ; v.t., to bear fruit.

sagi suffix to vb. : *livu, livusagi*. *sagini* trans. suffix to vb. : *livusagini*.

sagoi dehortative, used of sing. and pl. ; in more common use than *sa* 3 : (*o*) *sagoi matagu*, do not fear ! *koti sagoi piapilau*, do not steal ; used also as strong negative : *inau kuda sagoi mane piipisi*, I will not be a healer.

saininggi, to hasten, be quick.

saka 1, to paddle.

saka 2, to pluck fruit or flowers.

sakai, mutual, together, with one accord : *sakai godo*, a covenant, agreement ; *sakai hagore*, agreement ; *sakai hagoregi*, to make an agreement. Fl. *sakai*, one.

sakapa(gna), booth, shed, tent (late). *kasapa*.

saki, to step : *saki hadi*, to step up ; *saki hage*, step in, enter, embark.

sakoro, tight, not leaking, of boat.

sakuri v.t., to catch in the hands. Fl. *saku. sausaku*.

sanggala, to be empty, cleared of everything. (*saasanggala*). *vasanggala* v.t., to empty, clear out.

sanggi v.t., to tear in pieces, to rend the limbs. Fl. *sanggi*. (*saisanggi*).

salage numeral, ten ; used to denote a great number : *salage i thaba*, all kinds, numerous ; *na komi salage i thaba tango*, numerous works ; *e salage ngiha*, how many tens ! how numerous ! *sa* 1.

salagegna, tenth.

vasalage, ten times.

vasalagegna tenth.

salala, to shed, spill, of liquid : *bea sasalala*, running water. M. *sale* ; R. *ale*.

sale v.t., to sing ; a song : *salea na sale*, to sing a song ; *sale tangi*, the men's funeral chant ; *sale thaba*, to praise in song.

salemage, to be clear, of water.

salingau, a vision, apparition.

salu, polished, smooth.

salupa, to fail, be exhausted, of water or food, to heal, of ulcer : *ke salupa na bali vanga itanggua*, I have no food left ; *salupa pisupaa*, the very last one gone ; *hangga salupa*, almost all gone. *vasalupa* v.t., to cause to fail. *veisalupagi*, to be exhausted.

salusu, to slip, slide. (*sausalusu*).

sama, fibre for making string. S. *sämu*.

sami, to hasten. Fl. *samisami*.

saisami, be quick! hurry up! adv., quickly; precedes vb.

samingi v.t., to hasten, to go or do quickly or immediately.

samo, to clear away small growths preparatory to planting yams.

sani v.t., to leave; used as prep. of motion from: *toga sani*, to forgive; *na taviti saniagna*, departure, leaving; *thehe sasani*, a widow. Fl. *sani*.

sasani v.t., to divorce.

veisasanigi, to divorce.

saosagoma, rubbish, refuse.

saosaporagi, to slander.

sapa 1, to arrive, come, come to pass, to go down seawards: *au sapa*, to depart; *tuva sapa*, to launch a boat; *atu sapa*, to reach, arrive; *sapada*, let us go to the beach; *ke sapa na kalai* (*karango*), the tide ebbs. Fl. *sapa*; V. *japa*.

sapa 2, points along the coast.

sapa jae, a wind.

sape(*gna*), stage, shelf, seat, table, bed, plank: *sape i vunagi*, throne. Fl. *sape*.

sapi v.t. 1, to divide, be divided, desolate. Fl. *sapi*.

vasapi v.t., to divide.

sapi 2, an orphan; *sapigna*, to lack.

sapila, to let drop.

saporagi, to toss in a rough sea, of canoe, to jump the surf. (*saosaporagi*).

sapu, to profane, pollute, defile: *vele sausapu*, to blaspheme.

vasapu v.t., to corrupt.

sara 1, under, beneath, below, of place only; keel of canoe; the locative *i* generally precedes, and the pronouns of possession are suffixed: *i saragna*, *i sasaragna*, underneath (it); *sara i vathe*, under the house. Fl. *sara*.

sara 2, to go ashore, be aground; beach, strand. L. *hara*.

vasara v.t., to head for the shore, from sea.

saraka, to snare, noose, be caught in a snare; a snare, noose.

saraki v.t., to seize, lay hold of.

sari v.t., to make. Fl. *sari*.

sasari v.t., to hew, carve.

sari utu v.t., to overtake, go ahead, head off, intercept. *utu*. Fl. *sari*.

saropagini: *vele*(*ngele*) *saropagini*, to sneer at.

sasaa, to be active, diligent, busy: *sasaa piro*, to be zealous; *tango sasaapiro*, to be zealous; zeal. V. *jaza*.

sasaalagini v.t., to be zealous about, daring.

sasaa langagi, with power, to have the advantage over.

sasaba, to wrap food in leaves ready for cooking.

sasaka, leaf of sago palm.

sasalababa, disorderly.

sasamama, to howl.

sasara, midway, halfway up a hill.

sasigi, to strip off bark of tree, to plane a board.

sausaku, to answer back, defend oneself when accused, to excuse oneself. *sakuri*.

veisausakugi, to defend one another.

sausaube: *hai sausaube*, *ni sausaube*, to be wanton in behaviour.

sausavu, cloudy, hazy.

saveo, to be lame, falling to one side, not level.

savera v.t., to hang. Fl. *savera*. (*saesavera*).

savu v.t., to shut, close : *bilaki savu*, to shut out ; *ponoti savuni*, to shut up tight. Fl. *savu*.

savulagini v.t., to hurl, throw.

savusolu, clumsy, rough, ungentle.

sebe, to rot. Fl. *sebe*.

seka v.t., to take a person prisoner in a raid ; a captive, prisoner : *tinoni seka*, a captive, slave. Fl. *seka*.

sela, to store up almond nuts in a *binara*, to store generally.

selau : *sulupu selau*, to swim under water. *sulupu*.

selebange v.t., to weary, bore.

seli, armlet.

selo, English ' sail '

selima, to wash the hands. *lima*.

seo, reed.

seosedo, stones used in cooking. Fl. *sodesode*.

sepe, war dance.

sesehu(gna), feather, hair, grass.

sesere, to inlay with nautilus shell.

sesese, a bird, a swallow.

sesu v.t., to tear, rend.

sethe, to be many, much : *boi sethe*, not many ; *boi rae sethe*, not very many ; *boi gathi sethe*, less still ; *sethegna* much.

    vasethe v.t., to collect, accumulate.

sethevu(gna), beyond, on further side : *sethevu i kalai*, beyond the reef. *thevu*.

seu, a well, cup. Fl. *seu*.

seuselu v.t., to entice, deceive, cheat.

si 1, trans. suffix to vb. : *nggarusi*. Fl. *si*.

si 2, indefinite pron., used with *na* 1, a, a certain, another, one ... another, every, several : *si na mane*, a certain man, any man, a different man. *sikei*. L. *si*.

sia, bone arrow head.

siasigai, to carry in a sling.

sibi, to emit an odour, stink. R. *hibi*.

sidiri, to splash, sprinkle.

sido v.t., to profane.

sigo v.t., to look, to visit. Fl. *sigosigo*. (*siosigo*).

sigoagna gerund.

sigovi v.t., to visit.

sikei numeral, one, another, any one, a, the first; the one ... the other, each : *sikei na vula*, a new moon ; *sikei vamua*, only one, it doesn't matter, it's all one and the same ; *ke sikei*.

siesikei, one, one by one.

sikeigna : *na salage sikeigna*, the eleventh.

sikili, to drop, fall, let fall. S. *siki*. *vasikili* v.t., to let fall, drop.

sikodofu, to pilfer.

sikomi v.t., to take, gather, collect. S. *si'o*; Fl. *sikomi*. (*siosikomi*).

sikopo, to pilfer, pick at food.

singgo, to crack an almond in several blows. Fl. *singgo*.

silada, to shine ; brightness, glory (late). V. *silahi*, to lighten. (*siasilada*).

silibio, to slide out of, slip off. *vasilibio* v.t., to let slip off.

silikata, stone hammer for cracking almonds.

sili koakoba to be deceitful.

sinanggi(gna), lip.

sinathagi(gna), likeness.

sinathanggi(gna), nature. *thanggi*.

sinavera, peg, nail.

singimi me sangana, dispersed, of people, scattered, disunited.

sipa v.t., to extract, draw out from the body, pull out a plug. U. *sipa*.

masipa adj., come out of its own accord.

sipagna gerund.

sira, to bind, tie.

siraku, a ring, a button. Fl. *siraku*.

siraoraho, to drizzle.

sirapa, to itch.

siri v.t., to roast fish or flesh on embers or hot stones, to burn, fry (late). (*siisiri*).

siria passive, burnt.

siriki v.t., to burn.

siriu, to hate; used with *ni* 1.

siisiriuana v.n., abomination, abominable.

siriuhagi(ni) v.t., to despise, abhor.

siro, to look at. Fl. *siro*.

siromi v.t., to visit.

sisi, to be red. Fl. *sisi*.

sisimi, to drizzle, light rain. Fl. *simisimi*.

siu, to bathe, wash oneself. Fl. *siu*. (*siusiu*).

siuvi v.t., to wash, of feet : *siuvi tabu*, to baptize (late).

siuviagna gerund.

veisiuvi, to wash one another.

siuli, to swing.

sivarere, to run with the waves, of canoe.

sivi, a bird : *ke tangi na sivi*, when the *sivi* cries, the time just before dawn.

sivi ole, to flutter, of falling leaves, birds.

siviri onomatop., a red parrot. S. *siiri*.

soara, to be in flood ; a flood.

soaravi v.t., to flood.

soaravia passive, flooded.

soaraviagna gerund.

sobo v.t., to sit, place, stow, launch a canoe, lay up in the mind. Fl. *sobo*.

sobu, to stutter.

sodu, to be upright, perpendicular, straight ; the middle finger is *sodu* to the forearm. V. *hoto*.

soe 1, palsy, hemiphlegia. Fl. *soe*.

soe 2, paint.

soesole, to be naked, of males. *soleana*. Fl. *soesole*.

sogo 1, to play, jump, of fish.

sogo 2, in succession, successively ; to stay in turns with co-wives, of husband : *sogo i sapa*, points on coast opening out one after another.

sogovi v.t., to disperse.

soisoi, sap, discharge from ulcer. Fl. *soisoi*.

soisopi v.t., to nuzzle, kiss.

soisopiagna gerund.

veisoisopigi, to kiss one another.

soka, to impale, play cup and ball.

sosoka, to tabu a place, setting up a mark on a stick.

sokara, to stand up, rise; n., pillar, post, centre post of house, mast.

vasokaragini v.t., to set up, raise up.

sokara lau, a south wind. *sokara.*

sokiare, a garden weed. Fl. *sokiare*

soku(gna), side, loins.

songgala, to jump, spring up, rise, of sun : *songgalagna na aho*, sunrise. Fl. *soga.* (*soasonggala*).

songgalavi v.t., to jump at.

songgalaviagna gerund.

songge, to be bad, corrupt. (*soesongge*).

songgi v.t., to cut : *songgi vaugithatha*, to circumcise (late) ; *bali songgi*, blade of knife. Fl. *songgi.*

sola, a calm : *kutu sola*, singleness of heart.

soleana, peace, undisturbed conditions : *rei soleana*, to distinguish, see clearly. *soesole.*

veisoleanagi, to be at peace with one another.

soni v.t., to throw, put : *soni rongo*, to pay money, spend, make a monetary gift ; *soni haidu*, to meet together ; a gathering ; *soni orooro*, to take soundings ; *soni tuta*, to gain ; gains. Fl. *soni.*

soniagna gerund.

soni hathavu, to make a free gift, grant ; free grace (late).

sono, to swallow : *sono langgo*, to swallow whole ; *matha i sono*, a measure, finger tips to throat. S. *ono* ; Fl. *sono.*

sonovi v.t.

soosono(gna), throat (internal).

soosolo, side, of house.

sopa indefinite pron., each, every ; apart, different : *sopa thanggi*, different sexes, boy and girl twins ; *sopa hathangatu na thanggi*, by hundreds ; *e onoono*

soasopa na alodia, they had six wings apiece ; *sopa mono*, to be separate ; *hagore soasopa*, to disagree in speech ; *tagna sopa na vike*, in every family ; *havi sopa*, only begotten. Fl. *sopa* ; R. *hope.*

soparaka, dispersed, scattered. *sopa.*

vasoparaka v.t., to put to flight, scatter.

sope(gna), navel. Fl. *sope.*

sopou, to sit. Fl. *sopou.* (*sousopou*).

sopougna v.n., sitting.

vasopou v.t., to seat, set down.

sopu, to strike. Fl. *sopuku.*

sopulagi, to raise up, erect.

soropi v.t., to absorb liquid.

sosolagi, to flow, of tide.

sosolo(gna), foundation, bottom.

sosoloho(gna), id.

sosonota, to hiccough.

sosoro, canoe without raised ends. L. *sorosoro.*

sota, to fast, through grief or in sickness ; a fast.

soto, to be steady, still, calm, of sea, to stop short. (*soosoto*).

vasoto v.t., to silence.

sotha, black ant. Fl. *sola.*

sousopu : *dorovi sousopu* ; to gaze steadily at.

sua, to go backwards, retire. Fl., U. *sua.*

suaragi to retire, withdraw, to backwater.

veisuaragini v.t., to dissuade from a course of action.

sualilo, to turn round. *sua.*

sualo, to support, hold up a person.

suanogo, orphan.

suanura, hill.

suasula, to beguile, guileful, deceitful, to be a traitor.

suasupa(gna), hill, mountain.

suato, to lean, rest upon, trust.
suasuato, to limp.

suba v.t., to pierce, prick, spear.
suasuba, to spear fish.
subagna gerund.

subulo, to rush, scamper.

suesungge : *teteri suesungge*, to stand on tiptoe.

suge, to drive, of action of surf.

sugi, to follow a channel inside a reef. Fl. *sugi*.

suki, to pierce, impale, prick. Fl. *suki*.
susuki, to sew, thread, of fish-teeth or money beads.
susukiagna gerund.

suku, many.

sungga prep., within, in : *sungga i vathe*, in the house ; the locative *i* may precede. Nggao, Isabel, *sungga*, house.

sunggasarau, scattered, dispersed.

sula, to comfort, refresh ; used with *ni* 1.

sulagna v.n., comfort, refreshment.
vasula v.t.
veisuasualagi, to comfort one another.

suleke(gna), loins.

sulupagini v.t., to impale, insert, sheathe. Fl. *sulupa*.

sulupu, to enter, go through ; a channel, entrance, passage : *sulupu selau*, to dive ; *suusulupu*, to penetrate ; *rei suusulupu*, to see through a thing, as a window : *sulupungi* v.t., to go through.

sumari : *au sumari* v.t., to go through.

sune, to blow.

supa(gna), staff, rod, walking stick : *supa lee i bopa*, handle of digging stick.

supu, a large basket. Fl. *supu*.

sura, a fighting raid. Fl. *sura*.

suruku, to go up inland.

suruperere, to fall to pieces, of ill-tied bundle.

susa(gna), dew.

susunggula(gna), sweat ; to sweat.

susuru, diarrhœa. R. *huru* ; Fl. *suru*.

susuu(gna), woman's breasts, milk ; to suck the breast : *susuu hathavu*, to wean. Mel. *susu*.
suuvi v.t., to suck the breast.
vasuu v.t., to suckle.

sutu 1, v.t., to carry on the head, wear, of cap.
susutuagna gerund.

sutu 2, to prop up, stay ; a prop, stay.

suu v.t., to drive.

suusuu v.t., to hiss at. V. *suu*.
suusuuhagini v.t.

T

ta 1, prep., denotes general relationship, from, at, in, of, with ; the pronouns of possession are always suffixed : *tanggua, tamua, tagna, tada*, etc. : *tagna*, when, while ; *tagna iaani*, herein ; *tagna iangeni*, then. *ita*. Fl. *ta*.

ta 2, verbal noun suffix : *dikata* ; *toketa*.

ta 3, prefix to vb., denotes condition : *tanggumu* ; *tavuge.* M. *ta.* (*tata*).

taataha, few ; to be unfruitful, unsuccessful.

taba 1, sea shore. *i taba.* V., *taba.*

taba 2, v.t., to pay ; wages, reward, price. Fl. *taba.*

tabili, wooden mortar. Fl. *tabili.*

tabilolo, the rhinoceros beetle. Fl. *tabelulu.*

tabiru, to return ; adv., back ; followed by *i* 3 denoting ' turn into ', ' become ' ; has a reflexive use. Fl. *tabiru.* (*taitabiru*).

tabirua adv., again.

tabo 1, v.t., to touch, grope, take hold of, lay hands on. Fl. *tabo.* (*taotabo*).

taboagna gerund.

tabo 2 : *halu tabo,* disorderly conduct.

tabolo, a log, beam. Fl. *bubulo.*

tabu, to be sacred, forbidden, holy ; a prohibition placed on use or handling of anything. Fl. *tabu.*

vatabu v.t., to make *tabu.*

tabulo, suddenly. V. *tabulosi.*

tabulohagini v.t., to come upon suddenly.

tada 1, to look up ; adv., up : *rei tada,* to lift up the eyes ; *tada hadi,* to look up. R., Fl., *tada* ; L. *ada.*

vatada v.t., to raise up, set up, turn right way up, to set one's shield against an enemy.

tada 2, to be shallow, of pit or vessel.

tadakola, nearly full. *tada* 2.

tae(*gna*), excrement. M. *tae.*

taenggo v.t., to tend, care for, adopt.

veitaenggogi, to cherish mutually.

tafi 1, numeral, one.

tafi 2, kernel.

tafo v.t., to meet, intercept, keep a tryst.

tafu v.t., to cover, shade, protect with a covering.

tafuagna gerund.

tafungi v.t.

tautafugna v.n., a covering.

tafuni v.t., to kindle, light, of fire.

tafuru v.t., to add to, increase, spread over. (*tautafuru*).

tafuruagna gerund.

tagao, to steer, guide, set on a course ; steer oar, rudder : *mane tagao,* steersman. Fl. *tagao.*

tagaolagini v.t.

tagi v.t., to pluck hair or feathers.

tagini trans. suffix to vb. : *boitagini.* S. *ta'ini.*

tago, fish-hook. Fl. *tago* ; V. *tataho.*

taotago, to fish with a hook.

tagomo : *thehe tagomo,* to die of cold.

tahi(*gna*) 1, man's brother, woman's sister. M. *tasiu.*

tahi, 2, sea, salt water, salt : *tahi maha,* open sea. M. *tas* ; Fl. *tahi.*

taitahiga adj., salty, saltness ; to pour salt water on, to season with salt.

tahi 3, a vessel for holding salt-water.

tahotha, to accuse of infidelity. *tahotha lio,* to be jealous ; jealousy. *lio.*

tahu 1, to be heavy.

tahu(gna) 2, noise.

taitagi, to strike a fish, play a hook.

taitanggi, the cross-bar of a pump drill.

taitali paki, to exact money. U. *tari*, gain.

taitangi, to lever, prise.

taka, to spin ; a spinning top made of seed of barringtonia. Fl., R. *taka*.

takala(gna), scalp.

tanggi v.t., to weed.

tanggoti adj., broken. *nggotihi*. (*taotanggoti*).

tanggumu, to crash, of thunder. *nggumu*. Fl. *tanggumu*.

talangi v.t. to lead, conduct, convey : *talangi au*, to lead out from. S. *talai*.

talangiagna gerund.

talapono secretly, unawares. *pono*.

taliao, a clearing in forest, garden.

talu v.t., to put, place, appoint ; used as auxiliary verb to denote continuance of action ; adv., at all : *talu hagore*, to promise ; *talu vata*, to pledge ; pledge, debt, debtor ; *talu magavu*, to appoint a day ; *talu havi*, to be in good health ; *talu nago*, to be proud ; *talu legu*, to be humble ; *talu polo*, to hide, secrete ; *talu mono*, to abide, stay on ; *talu tavoga*, to forgive ; *talu thehe*, to be dead for good ; *nia talu sokara*, to keep on standing. Fl. *talu* ; L. *alu*. (*tautalu*).

talua exclam., stop ! wait a minute ! refrain !

taluagi v.t., to put.

taluagini v.t., to ambush, lie in wait for, to watch a net.

taluagna gerund., placing, putting, appointing.

talugau, to cut.

talugu, outside, the outside of, back : *i talugu* ; *talugugna*, the outside of it.

tama(gna) 1, father. Mel. *tama*.

tama 2, prefix used with relationship terms to denote sets of people : *tamatahi*, brethren, sisters, family ; *ara gada tamatahi*, our family ; *tamadathe*, set of children, family. Fl., R. *tama*.

tamaga, to inherit, inheritance. Fl. *tamaga*.

tamaji, to eat flesh food as a relish with vegetables: *hagore tamaji*, to speak in a mixed fashion, pidgin English. S. *amadi*.

tamathagi, to entrust, commit to a person's care.

tamathagini v.t., to deliver over.

tano 1, earth, ground. M. *tano*.

tano 2 : *hatha tano* v.t., to collect. *hatha*.

tanuvi v.t., to dip, soak in water.

tangi, to cry, cry aloud, lament, wail ; n., crying, lamentation : *tangi mate*, to wail ; *sale tangi*, to cry aloud ; *tangi kiri*, the lamentation over a corpse. Mel. *tangi*. (*taitangi*).

tangihi v.t., to desire, want, to bewail.

tango, to perform, do, work ; n., deeds : *tango vahotha*, to toil ; *tango poopolo*, to play the hypocrite, deal deceitfully ; *bali tatango*, a tool, a handle. Fl. *tango*.

tangoli v.t., to take, to hold, handle, receive : *tangoli hadi*, to feel for a thing.

tangoagna, *tangoliagna*, gerund. *veitangogi*, to work at a thing mutually.

tango malaga, *tango mana*, to be able, able to do ; followed always by a gerundive: *ke tango mana na ijumiradiagna*, able to count them. *tango* ; *mana*. Fl. *tangomana*.

tangopara,to be beautiful to look at.

tao, ridge, saddle of mountain, pass : *tao hathavu*, a measure, finger tips to further shoulder ; *labu tao*, to nail crosswise. Fl. *tao*.

taofi, to set, place, lay hands on, touch.

taofiagna gerund.

taotapo, dragon fly. *tapo.*

tapa, to tread lightly, step ; a step : *bali taatapa*, footstool ; *taatapa i thonga*, to land from a canoe.

veitaatapaligi, to tread on one another.

tapalao, old name for ship.

tapeleku, to slide, slip.

tapo v.t., to strike, clap, of hands. S. *tapo*. (*taotapo*).

tapori v.t., to break off with the hand.

tapoto, to continue doing, be persistent, to pay frequent visits to a place.

tapurese, to bud, be open, of eye. V. *tavurese*.

vatapurese v.t., to cause to bud.

tarago, to crouch, lurk.

tarai, to pray ; prayer. R., Fl. *tarai*.

taraju, to slip, slide.

tarakusu v.t., to cut off a piece, amputate. *kusu*.

taraoa, yellow land snail.

tarariju, a slip knot.

tari v.t., to bind, tie : *tari ulu*, a head fillet. Fl. *tari*. (*tatari*).

tarongi v.t., to possess, of demoniacal possession, the person so possessed pines away. (*taotarongi*).

tarunga(gna), soul, spirit : *tarunga i kilo*, echo. Fl. *tarunga*.

tarutata, easy, elemental.

tasu v.t., to stroke, anoint. *tautasuagna* gerund.

tata verbal prefix denoting condition : *tatanggutu*. *ta* 3.

tataba i lima, a hand's breadth, the palm of the hand.

tatabala, to cross over, go over. *baabala*.

tataji, careful : *hati tataji*, to receive, accept, entertain. (*taatataji*).

tatanggutu, to assemble in crowds, to crowd. *tata*.

tatarai raki, to scratch, pluck out, pull and tear.

tate, to show ; adv., openly : *tate au*, to show, explain ; *tuturi tate*, to bear witness. Fl. *tate*.

tateli v.t., to publish, show, tell. *tateliagna* gerund.

tatohu v.t., to break in pieces, be broken. (*taotatohu*).

tatha, a crowd, war party in canoes, enemy : *mara ganggua na tatha*, my enemies. L. *tasa*, excess.

tathahi, to spin.

tatho, webbed, of birds' feet.

tau(gna), wife, husband. Fl. *tau*.

taulagi, to marry : *vaivine taulagi*, bride ; *mane taulagi*, bridegroom ; *taulagi paru*, to be betrothed.

taudolu, whole, complete, perfect. *udolu*.

vataudolu v.t., to make perfect, complete.

tautamuhi v.t., to wave, shake, strike, flick, flap.

tautau, to stay, sojourn : *tautau vathe*, to keep to the house.

tautu, to cut off, be broken short off, finished : *gagana tautu*, to be decided, of mind ; *tautu i gai*, a billet of wood. Fl. *tautu*.

vatautu v.t., to finish off.

tava, verbal prefix denoting spontaneity. M. *tava*.

tavaguguri, to blow in gusts ; a gust of wind. *guri*.

tavaha, to be freed, to break through, be open, of mouth of stream.

vatavaha v.t., to open, free, dissipate, of mist.

tavangguluva, weak, faint with hunger, famished. *ngguluva*.

tavalili v.t., to leave, set aside, depart, refuse in anger. *lilihi*.

tavararaha, enlightened, cleared, of mind. *tava*.

tavate, to clear after rain, of weather.

tavauunu, loosed. *tava*.

tave v.t., to shed, of blood, to flow. S. *ahe* ; Fl. *tave*. (*taetave*).

tatave, to float.

tavea passive, shed.

taveagna gerund.

taviti, to go, walk : *taviti tavoga*, to get out of the way ;

na taviti saniagna, departure. (*taitaviti*).

tavitigna v.n., going.

tavoga, different, others, the rest : *imarea tavoga*, the others ; *halu tavoga*, to be contrary in behaviour. *voga*. Fl. *voka*, divided.

vataotavoga v.t., to make otherwise.

tavotha adj., wide. M. *tavola*.

tavuge, to blow, of wind ; the rushing of wind : *tavuge magavu*, a squall, tempest ; *na magavu ke tavuge mai*, a fierce squall came. *ta* 1 ; S. *hu'e*, to open.

tavuli, conch shell used as trumpet : *ifu tavuli*, to blow the trumpet. Fl. *tavuli* ; S. *ahuri*.

tavuru v.t., to sprinkle with water or powder.

tea, spider's web. V., Fl. *tea*.

teku, ulcer.

tengge, the tortoise-shell barb of a bonito hook.

tengguru, house.

tengedeu, rat-trap. Fl. *tengedeu*.

tena 1, fishing net.

tena 2, to sew sago palm leaves for thatch, to weave, of spider.

teo negative, not to be, no.

teoa adj., gone, destroyed, wanting, not to be : *hangga teo*, hardly, scarcely ; *iso teoteoa*, the least.

vateo v.t., to destroy.

vateoagna gerund.

teri, to step : *teteri i thonga*, to land from a canoe ; *teteri suesungge*, to walk on tiptoe.

terihi v.t., to walk.

tete, to climb up on a fishing tripod. Fl. *tete.*

teve, to be long, tall.

tevegna v.n., length.

ti 1, trans. suffix to verb : *pono, ponoti.*

ti 2, component part of v.p. *ati, iti, oti, timara, timarea* ; probably *vati,* four, used to express ' many '.

tidatho, ghost, amulet : *mane tidatho,* magician. Fl. *tidalo* ; S. *akalo.* (*tiatidatho*).

tietinggele, coastal cliff.

tifi, to break off.

tigo, used to translate ' horn ' ; probably piece of coconut husk left on shell for tying.

tihi v.t., to dip into water, wash. Fl. *tihi.*

tihigi v.t., to plait, weave (*tiitihigi*).

tiho(*gna*), beginning.

tiitili, stone wall ; to build a stone wall. Fl. *tiitili.*

tinggehi, shallow water.

tila, a wooden club. Fl. *tila.*

tilima, to pour out, sprinkle. (*tiitilima*).

tilo, a sloughing ulcer.

timara, timarea, they. *ti* 2.

tina(*gna*), mother. Fl., V. *tina.*

tinabe, weapons. Fl. *tinabe.*

tinarai v.t., to teach, instruct, to mediate. R. *tinarai.*

   veitinaraigi, to instruct one another.

tinathagi : *halu tinathagi,* to be wise.

tinaulu(*gna*), chief, head. *ulu.*

tinoga, tribute money, paid to keep off enemies.

tinoho(*gna*), beginning, origin ; long time ago.

tinoni, man, mankind, person, male person : *tinoni hotha,* a slave, bought or captured ; *tinoni seka,* a captive slave ; *ninggua na tinoni,* one of my men ; *hai tinoni,* a stranger, chance comer ; *na tinonigna na meleha,* a man of the place ; *tinoni puhi,* adult. Fl. *tinoni* ; S. *inoni.*

tiotinoni, foundation logs of house, a pile.

tiro, to look ; a pool, window glass, mirror : *na bali tiro,* a looking glass. S. *iroiro.*

tita, the putty nut. Fl. *tita.*

titiono, to tell a story, proclaim, preach ; report, story, folk-lore tale : *na titionogna a Kamakajaku,* the story of Kamakajaku.

toa(*gna*) 1, hill fortress. R. *toa,* mountain peak.

toa 2, to be tired, weary, idle.

   toali, to be lazy.

tobi v.t., to fell a tree, clear the bush.

tobolo, wet through, sopping.

toe, to put an enchantment on a person, generally by using complimentary words ; an enchantment. (*toetoe*).

toga(*gna*) 1, man's elder brother, woman's elder sister. Fl. *tuga.*

toga 2, to think : *toga tabiru,* to remember; *toga sani,* to forget, forgive; *toatoga,* to meditate.

toga 3, numeral, thousand : *na toga.* Fl. *toga* ; V. *toha.*

togahi v.t., to cover, spread over.

togi v.t., to loose, undo, destroy. Fl. *togi.*

togo, to add. *togolo.* Fl. *togo.*

togokale, certain, sure : *ado togokale*, to know for certain : *rei togokale*, to witness, see clearly. *kathe* ; Fl. *kale*.

togolo, to add. *togo*.

togoloa adj., in abundance.

togoni : *horu togoni*, to arrive, of an appointed day.

togulu, multitude, crowd : *togulu i vula*, strangers arriving. Fl. *togulu*.

toi(gna) 1, the left hand.

toi 2, to draw water, dip and fill a water-vessel, to water a plant. Fl. *toi*. (*toitoi*).

toilo v.t., to twist, plait into a ring.

toka v.t., to fell a tree, to chop down. Maori, *toka*, axe ; Fl. *toka*. (*toatoka*).

totoka, a hoe (late).

toke, good, that will do ! enough ! come now ! well then ! ; to be beautiful, of a woman : *na toke*, goodness ; *e hava rae tokegna*, how beautiful ! *nau tovongai tokenggu*, till I am well. Fl. *toke*.

toetokelagagna gerund., to be excellent.

toketa-(gna) v.n. : *na toketanggu*, I am glad.

vatoke v.t., to benefit, bless (late).

veitokegi, to be friends again.

tokuvi v.t., to rest upon, cover, of mist or cloud.

tongga, to be quiet, silent, assured in mind : *mono tongga*, be quiet ! behave ! *hehe i tongga*, confident.

tonggotonggo, to rejoice, be glad ; *tootonggo*, to rejoice ; joy, gladness. Fl. *tonggo*.

tola, large canoe with prow and stern not very high. V. *tola*.

tolira, they three, of men only.

toliira, they three, of women only.

tolojo v.t., to fill one vessel from another, to conceive.

tolu numeral, three : *sikei na toludia na tango*, they three had the same occupation ; *na tolu naemiu*, the legs of you three. The following pronominal forms contain *tolu*, being used of three persons : *tolugami, tolugamu, tolugita, tolu iraani, tolumaraira, tolumarea*. Fl. *tolu*.

tolugna, third.

tolumara, you ! of address to a number.

vatolui, third, third time.

vatolugna, third.

vitolu, the third day, back or forward, not counting to-day : *vitolu na magavu*, three clear days.

tomaga, excess, surplus, over and above : *e lima tomaga*, five and more ; *e salage me tomaga*, ten and some over.

tomoko, war canoe. R. *tomoko*.

tona, to abuse in speech : *vele tona*, to revile.

toni 1, rocky, stony, of ground.

toni 2, possibly, perhaps ; follows a verb. *tuni*.

toni 3, urgently, insistently ; precedes a verb.

tono(gna) 1, body. Fl. *tono*.

tono 2, to have, possess : *miti tonomami na komi fata*, we possess the things ; *ke tononga*, his possessions.

tono 3, possessions : *na tononggu na komi fata iaani*, these things are mine.

tongari v.t., to abuse, ill use, rebuke, scold, threaten. (*toatongari*).

tongariagna, gerund.

tootogo i vathe, verandah. *togo*.

tootoo, areca palm.

topa, a fish : *sikei na boka i topa*, ten *topa*.

totoola, certainty, the absolute truth : *rei totoola*, to see for a certainty ; *hagore totoola*, to bear witness.

tora, to be phosphorescent. Fl. *tora*.

toro 1, v.t., to accuse, bear witness.

toroagna, gerund.

veitootorovigi, to accuse one another.

veitorovigi, to make cross accusations.

toro 2, to put, place.

torongagi, to continue straight on, reach : *torongagi sethevu*, to cross over ; *torongagi tuturu*, to kneel.

toroko, the erection on stem or stern of canoe : *toroko nago* ; *toroko legu*.

tororo, to lower, let down, descend, sink, drown. Fl. *dororo*.

toto, verbal prefix denoting spontaneity : *totopiti*. S. *toto*.

totobei v.t., to clear, of path.

totonggo, mud.

totovagi, to shout ; a shout.

totopiti, to revolve ; a wheel.

totopo, a pipe.

totha v.t., to touch, to light a candle.

totho, to be placed end to end, to join, be firm, weighty, of words ; a joint.

toototho, to hunt for yams or taros in ground already dug : *vanga toototho*, the first meeting of two parties to make friends.

vatotho v.t., to join, fix firmly, graft.

toukake, clearly, carefully ; follows a vb. : *tango toukake*, to do carefully.

tove : *mono tove*, to abide, stay continuously. Fl. *tove*.

tovongai, tovongoi, until, when, as soon as ; precedes a vb. ; the conj. *nggi* may precede the pers. pron. used as subject : *mu ku tovongai hagore vanigo*, until I tell you ; *nggi u tovongoi regia na hava ke pada*, until I see what will happen.

tovu, to be satisfied, supplied, to have one's share. V. *tovu*.

vatovu v.t.

tovuhi v.t., to spread over, as ulcer, fire, etc., to swarm over, lay over.

tua : *tua varava*, to rest upon or against, lean, incline, trust. Fl. *tua*, leg.

tualagi tuturu, to rest the knee on the ground, kneel.

tuali, old, of an article.

tubi, a tree, ebony. V. *tubi*, staff.

tubu 1, to swell ; a simple ulcer, an ulcerous person, leper (late) : *tubu gahira*, boils. S. *upu*. (*tulubu*).

tubu(gna) 2, mother's brother, sister's son, of a man. Fl. *tubu*.

tubutha, a crab.

tudu, to drip, of water or tears ; a drop. S. *udu.* (*tuutudu*).

tuduhi v.t., to drip on to.

vatudu v.t., to let drip.

tufali v.t., to distribute.

tugu v.t., to change, exchange, barter : *tugu hehe*, to repent ; repentance ; *tugu kibo*, to repay a debt ; *tugu hagore*, to answer. Fl. *tugu.*

tuguagna gerund., in exchange for, instead of.

tuguva v.n. : *tuguva oli*, interchange, alternate, turn and turn about ; *na tuguva*, exchange.

tuguni v.t., to guess, give a name to : *tuguni poto*, to tell a folklore tale ; *tuguni aha*, to give a name to. Fl. *tugu.*

tuguniagna, gerund.

Tuhilagi, the home of the dead.

tuhu, to stretch out the hand, point with the finger ; used with *ni* 1. Fl. *tuhu.*

tuhu liulivu, generous, bountiful. *livu.*

tuitugi, to strike with a quick blow.

tungge v.t., to touch, come in contact with, brush against. R. *tungge.*

tula, black bruise, scar.

tulu, to spread a mat.

tulungi v.t., to soak in water, leave in soak.

tuni, see *toni* 2.

tunu, a mark, blot, cicatrice caused by burning. M. *tun* ; S. *unu* ; R. *tunu.*

tuutunu, to be spotted.

tunuva, portion of food, land, etc., inheritance. Fl. *tunuva.*

tungi, large clam.

tuotulo, to get off the track in the dark, be perverse.

tupa, to be ripe, of coconuts or almonds. V. *tupa.*

tupi v.t., to beat, strike, hammer, stake : *bali tupi*, a hammer. Fl. *tupi.*

tupipuhi, a nail.

turabuto, white shell-money. Fl. *turabuto* ; V. *turubuto.*

turu, to be dirty, unclean ; dirt. filth.

vaturu v.t., to defile, make dirty.

vaturuagna gerund.

turube, to drip, of fluid.

turugu, to begin ; followed by *i* 3 ; the beginning.

turugugna v.n.

tuta, to be thick, of plank, etc. : *tuta vano*, to grow bigger ; *soni tuta*, gain.

tutu v.t., to build, build up, with stone or wood, to make up a bed, lay one thing on top of another. Fl. *tutu.* (*tuututu*).

tutuagna gerund.

tutuana v.n., memorial.

tutuba, a passing squall.

tutugu(gna), a score, twenty : *mara e tutugu vati*, twenty-four people ; *e rua tutugu*, forty ; *tutugu sikei*, twenty-one ; *e tutugu lima*, twenty-five.

tutuguru, bush, shrub.

tutumu lio, to long after, hanker after, yearn after. *lio.*

tutuni, to be true : *na tutuni*, the truth, verily. *utuni.* V. *tutuni.*

tuturi v.t., to show, proclaim : *tuturi auagna*, proclaiming.

tuturu(gna), knee, joint : *tualagi tuturu*, to kneel. Fl. *tuturu* ; S. *uruuru.*

tuturube, to spurt out, pour downwards.

tuu 1, to be excited, dismayed, to sink, of heart.

tuu 2, to stand : *tuu vano*, exalted, more than (in comparison) ; *hava rae tuugna*, how much more ! Fl. *tu*.

tuutu 1, to throb, beat, of heart.

tuutu, 2, tenor bamboo pipe.

tuutufu v.t., to rebel against.

tuutulu, hot stones placed at bottom of oven on leaves.

tuutuu loalova, continuous, continuously. *tuu* 2.

tuutuu teeteve, continuous, continuously. *teve*.

tuva 1, to haul, propel, launch, push, pull.

   tuvati v.t., to detach creepers from tree, clear obstacles from path.

tuva 2, a creeper used for poisoning fish ; to poison fish.

Th

The sound of *th* is that of the soft English *th*. A *th* in Bugotu is often represented by an *l* in other Melanesian languages.

tha verbal noun suffix : *hagetha*.

thaba, great ; greatness : *salage i thaba*, everything, all things. M. *lava*.

   vathaba v.t., exalt, magnify.

thabota, to spread, of morning light ; morning light : *ke thabota*, when it was morning ; *nggi e pota na thabota*, when it was morning. Fl. *labota*.

thabu v.t., to smite, strike, kill, play on stringed instrument. S. *rapu* ; Fl. *labu*.

thabuhi v.t., to strike, kill, of persons.

thabuhiagna gerund.

veithauthabu, veithauthabuhigi, to strike, kill, one another.

thabuhagi, to blink, wink ; adv., suddenly, in the twinkling of an eye. *thabu*.

thabutu, mixed pus and blood.

thae v.t., to go towards ; used as prep. of motion towards : *na vano thaeagna*, to go to him. S. *lae*, to go.

thagi 1, verbal suffix : *kobathagi*.

thagi 2, v.t., to draw, pull.

thaho, to castrate. M. *laso*, scrotum.

   thaothaho, to be unfruitful, cast fruit, of tree, to be half-full.

   thaothahogna, unfruitful.

   thathaho, a gelding pig, eunuch (late).

thako, a charm, grass worn round neck to cure or ward off sickness.

thangga, to be steadfast, firm, confident ; confidence. Fl. *langga*.

   vathangga v.t., to confirm, strengthen, sustain.

   vathanggagna v.n., a confirming, strengthening.

thanggi, kind, sort, row, line : *na komi thanggi botho*, all kinds of beasts.

thamuta, corpse of person killed by violence : *thehe thamuta*, to die a violent death. Fl. *lamuta*.

thanu, to bale ; a baler. U. *danu*. *thanuti* v.t.

thango, a fly. Mel. *lango*.

thangu, to adhere, stick. Fl. *langgolanggo*.

thanguti v.t., to stick to.

vathanguti v.t., to pitch with pitch, daub.

vathangutiagna gerund.

thaothadoga, to know ; wisdom, understanding : *na bali thaothadogagna*, knowledge.

thaothao, to draw water.   ? M. *sao*.

thaopi v.t., to bale out, ladle, dip out.

thaopiagna gerund.

thaothapo, to boast.

thaotharo : *vanga thaotharo*, to eat vegetable food only.

thapi(gna), tongue. Fl. *lapi*.

thara v.t., to spread, scatter, straw. M. *sara*.

tharagna v.n.

thare, to be undecided about, doubt, wonder ; used with *ni* 1.

tharegna v.n.

thau v.t., to take by force, snatch. S. *lau* ; R. *zau*.

thauthamumu, to mark the time by clapping of hands when playing the pipes. Fl. *hamumu*.

thauthamumugna v.n.

thavi 1, v.t., to drive, of action of waves. M. *lav*.

thaithavi, flood, current.

thavi 2, to pluck out : *thavi kutu*, to gut. Fl. *lavi*.

thavi nago, first-fruits, first-born. *nago*.

thavu, to scatter, throw broadcast : *thavu hagore*, to talk incessantly. M. *savur*.

thego(gna), shoulder.

thehe, to die ; death : *thehe haihavi*, danger. (*thethehe*).

vathehe v.t., to strike, injure, kill, to pay for a thing, as canoe, house, etc.

vatheheagna gerund., killing, to kill, the price of.

vathehegna v.n., the price of.

thehe sasani, a widow, widower ; to be widowed. *thehe*.

thepa, the ground, floor, earth, mud : *i thepa*, below, on the ground, earthwards ; *maumauvu i thepa*, dust of the earth ; *i thepagna*, underneath (it), below. M. *lepa*.

thethenggura, to bear plentifully, of coconuts, etc.

theu, away, beyond : *theu vano*, over yonder, on beyond ; *theugna vano*.

theuthehu v.t., to mock, jest. *leuleu*.

thevu(gna), part, division, side : *thevugna*, beyond, other side, on far side ; *thevu i oka*, enemy ; used with *ga* 1. Fl. *levu*.

theuthevu v.t., to divide.

thevu lima, a measure, finger tips to nearer shoulder. *thevu*.

thevu rua, to separate, divide into two. *thevu*.

thevuruagna v.n.

thobio, ship worm, teredo.

thogu, to be lame. V. *lohu* ; S., Fl. *loku*.

thohi v.t., to contract, draw together, bend, of bow.

thoki, to be bent, curved, winding, crooked.

vathoki v.t., to bend, make into a curve.

vathokiagna gerund.

thonggo kama, name of a marriage clan : *posomogo* ; *vihuvunagi*.

thomati v.t., to consume, devour ; to deprive a person of all his possessions.

thonga, to go ashore ; ashore, from seawards : *saki thonga. longa.*

thoti v.t., to clasp, embrace, seize forcibly : *nere thoti*, to sleep soundly. Fl. *loti.*

thotiagna gerund.

thoto, pus.

thotho, red ant. S. *lolo.*

thothoho, to bathe. S. *loloto.*

thovo, to fly, leap : *thovo liungi*, the passover ; *thovo haliu*, to fly over, pass by ; adv., throughout. S. *loho.* (*thothovo*).

thovo haliugna v.n.

vathovo v.t., to blow away, cause to fly.

U

u, pers. pron., 1st pers. sing., I. *ku.*

uauro onomatop., to howl.

udolu 1, all, whole, complete, perfect, totality ; follows a noun.

udolu 2, to be all gathered together, of persons. *MIL.* 237, *otolu* ; M. *nol.* (*udoudolu*).

udolua adj.

udu, to guide, to companion with : *udu haidu*, to go together ; used with *ni* 1. Fl. *udu.*

uduudua v.n., companion, fellow traveller.

ufa, to be grey headed.

ufe, taro tops for planting.

uha, to rain ; rain. Fl. *uha.*

uiumi, to grunt, of pig.

ujatha, a flock of birds, shoal of fish, herd of pigs.

ujuri, to rub the skin, as when bathing. *gnujuri.* S. *usuri.*

unggura, to fish with a net.

ula(gna), tendon, sinew, vein. U. *ulaula* ; Fl. *ula.*

ulaga(gna), to be suitable, fit, becoming to. V. *ulaha* ; Fl. *ulaga.*

uli v.t., to let down, lower, sink, subside.

ulo, maggot. M. *ulo.*

uloa adj., maggoty.

ulu(gna), head, top, end : *tari ulu*, head fillet ; *ulu horu*, to bow the head, obey, recline, lean. Fl. *ulu.*

ulunga(gna), a pillow ; to pillow the head. *ulu.* M. *ulunga.*

umata, snake. Fl. id.

unga(gna), shade, shadow : *kutu i unga*, nightfall ; *unga i vathe*, verandah. Fl. *unga.*

ungahi v.t., to overshadow.

ungaunga(gna), shadow.

ugnu(gna), cast skin of snake.

ura, crawfish. Mel. *ura.*

urese, mucus.

uri, to perish, be lost sight of, to be overgrown, of path, ruined, of house. Fl. *uri.*

urio, crab, birgus latro.

uru, to hang.

urungu, to speak loudly, make a noise.

utu 1, adv., outwards, onwards ; *hatha utu*, path ; *sari utu*, to go ahead, overtake. Fl. *utu.*

utu 2, to build : *utu vathe*, to build a house.

utuhi v.t.

utuhiagna, building, to build.

utuhi v.t., to sever, cut off, cut in two, to finish building a house. *utuutu.*

utuni, to be true, true. *tutuni.*
    Fl. *utuni.*
vautuutuni v.t., to believe.
vautuutunia v.n., belief.
vautuutuniagna gerund.
utuutu, to clip, crop, cut short.
    utuhi.
utuutugna, v.n.
uunu, to be stripped off, stripped
    naked, undone, of knot.
    tavauunu.
uunuhi v.t., to undo.
uunuhia passive, loosed.
uunuhiagna gerund., to declare.
uvi, yam, generic term. S. *uhi.*
uvu, to be powdery, friable, open,
    of soil, floury. Fl. *uvu.*

V

va 1, verbal noun suffix : *tuguva.*
    M. *va.*
va 2, causative prefix to vb. :
    vahavi ; used with the
    numerals : *varuai* ; *varuagna.*
    M. *va.*
vaa, to open, of mouth, clasp-
    knife, box.
vaavaha, to whisper.
vaavanga, to be sharp. Fl. *vanga.*
vabobo v.t., to heap up.
vae(gna) 1, hip.
vae 2, to catch turtle with a net.
vaga, as. Fl. *vaga.*
    vagagna, like, as ; *ke vagamami
    igami*, like us ; *ke vagagna na
    manu*, like a bird.
vagi verbal suffix ; *ahavagi.* M.
    vag.
vagina, to reprove, correct.
vago, red scallop shell.
vagoda, to hunt for shell fish on
    the reef.   Maewo, New

Hebrides, *vangoda*, to catch
    fish.
vagu(gna), bundle, receptacle for
    clubs or spears. V. *vego* ; Fl.
    vauvagu.
    vauvagu, parcel ; to make a
    parcel of.
vahagi, to be ill. Fl. *vahagi.*
    (*vaavahagi*).
    vahagiti v.t., to be ill of.
    vahagitiagna gerund.
vahi v.t., to choose ; judge. Fl.
    vahi. (*vavahi*).
    vahiagna gerund.
vahingoto, a thorny creeper.
vaho adv., indeed, very, verily :
    vaho iangeni, that very time.
    Fl. *vaho.*
vahotha 1, to be difficult, costly,
    with difficulty, entangled. Fl.
    vahola.
vahotha 2, cliff, precipice.
    vahothagini,   to   be   costly,
    valuable.
vahu(gna) 1, forehead, temples :
    vahu i mata. Fl. *vahu* ; V.
    vasu.
vahu 2, to bring forth, give birth
    to : *vahu baso*, to bear twins.
    Fl. *vahu* ; M. *vasus.*
    vahuagna gerund.
    vahuhu v.t., to beget, of either
    parent.
vahui : *nago vahui*, the firstborn ;
    na vahuigna, the first. *vahu* 2.
    (*vahuihui*).
vaivine(gna), woman, female ;
    used to denote sex : *nggari
    vaivine*, girl. M. *tavine.*
    favaivine, to be effeminate.
vajangi v.t., to perceive, discern,
    feel, of cold, etc. Fl. *vadangi.*
    veivajangi, to be sympathetic.

vajovo v.t., to defraud, deceive, get by fraud.

vaka(gna), ship. Probably Mota *aka*.

valau, stone axe, steel axe.

vali v.t., to spread out, unfold, of mat, net, etc.; *vali utu*, to encompass.

valiagna gerund.

vavali v.t., to line the oven with leaves for cooking.

vavaligna v.n., lining of oven.

valiha, third day, past or to come, day before yesterday, day after to-morrow : *vugoi valiha*, in the future, time to come ; *valiha gohi*, three days ago. Fl. *valiha*.

valisavu v.t., to profane, transgress, violate, of holy places or things.

valuha, to paddle a canoe, row ; paddling.

vamoomogo v.t., to loosen.

vamua adv., only, merely, forsooth, indeed ; has explanatory use, ' I mean' : *sikei vamua*, it's all one and the same, it doesn't matter ! *va* 2. Fl. *vamua*.

vanete, cuscus opossum.

vani prep., to, of dative, for ; the pronouns of the object are always suffixed : *talu polo vania*, to hide from him ; *hatia mai vaniu*, bring it to me ; *na ijumi vaniagna*, a reckoning to him ; *me vania*, and said to him. Fl. *vani* ; S. *huni*.

vano, to go, come ; used in comparisons, beyond, more : *ke hutu vano*, it is bigger ; *vano*

me vano, more and more ; *ke sethe vano*, much more ; *tuu vano tagna*, more than ; *hujuu vanogna*, he has gone away ; used as auxiliary verb meaning ' to be ', ' go to ', ' about to ' : *vano he*, to give, about to give ; *koda vano nggotihira*, thou shalt break them. M. *van* ; Fl. *vano*. (*vavano*).

vano(gna), *vanoa* v.n., a journey, a going.

vanoi, to go, go to, come.

vano hehe, to desire, lust after ; desire, lust : *ena vanohehedia*, they desire ; *kori vido ku vanohehenggu*, at the time which I desired. *hehe*.

vanua, land, island. M. *vanua*.

vanga, to eat ; vegetable food : *hea na vangga*, give him some food ; *na bali vanga*, food ; *vanga tidatho*, septicæmia ; *na vido i vangagna na vunagi*, the king's food country. Fl. *vanga*.

vaavanga, crops, food.

vao v.t., to plait. Fl. *vao* ; M. *vau*.

vapulodo v.t., to scorch.

vara, to ascend in clouds, to smoke, of fire : *na ahu ke vara*, clouds of smoke.

varava, to lean, trust, rely : *koli varava*, to lean. Fl. *varava*.

vararava, to rely on, trust.

vari 1, prefix denoting reciprocity : *vari nanaba*, co-equal ; *i vari hotagigna i Bethel ma i Ai*, midway between Bethel and Ai. M. *var*.

vari(gna) 2, heir, heritage ; to inherit. Fl. *vavari*.

variapo, to toss about, be rough, of sea in a tide rip, place where two currents meet. *vari* 1.

varipuku 1, a knot; to tie up together. *puku* 1. Fl. *varipuku*.

varipuku 2, specific numeral, ten, of *buma* fish : *sikei na varipuku*, ten *buma* fish.

vataetae v.t., to assign, apportion, dispose of one's goods. *va* 2.

vatara, to stretch.

vatavaha v.t., to dissipate, of action of sun on mist, to let flow, of water.

vati, numeral, four : *mena thevu vatia*, and they made four parts of it. S. *hai*.

vaivati, four apiece.

vatigna, fourth. (*vavatigna*).

vatigo v.t., to send away, dismiss ; exclam., be gone !

vathe(gna), house : *vathe aava*, *vathe babale*, a shed. Fl. *vale* ; S. *hale*.

vathegila, specific numeral, ten million, of stored canarium almonds.

vaugithatha, a mark, sign. *githatha*. Fl. *vaugilala*.

vaura v.t., to save. *va* 1. S. *ha'auri* ; M. *maur*.

vautuutuni, see *utuni*.

vauvanggu, to be ready, prepared. Fl. *vanggu*, to tidy up.

vava, monitor lizard.

vavaha adv., merely, just, for no reason, naked, of sword, bareheaded : *hagore vavaha*, to whisper.

vavahu, to put a husked coconut on the fire.

vavaro v.t., to despoil ; spoils of war.

vavarogna gerund.

vavatara, to soar, fly, of bird.

vavine(gna), man's sister, woman's brother : *inau a vavinegna*, I am his sister. Fl. *vavine* ; M. *tavine*, woman.

vavotu v.t., to warn.

vavotuagna gerund.

vavugo, to arrive early at a place, to be early afoot. *vugoi*.

vavuru, to bait a trap, load a gun or pipe ; bait for fishing : *vavuruagna na tago*, to bait a hook.

veavela, to speak loudly, shout a message.

veavelagna v.n.

veevene, to be firm, stable, obstinate, stubborn.

vei 1, verbal prefix denoting reciprocity ; the suffix *gi* is generally added to the compound word : *veijukagi* ; *koti veimono soleana*, be at peace with one another ; the compound word may be used as a noun : *veidothovigi*, mutual love. Fl. *vei* ; S. *häi*. (*veivei*).

vei 2, adv., where ? anywhere ; used with *i* 2 prefixed : *ivei mivei*, here and there. M. *vei* ; S. *itei*.

veikurikurigi, to dispute, altercate. *vei* 1.

veinigi, mutually : *koti veinigi tango na dotho*, serve one another in love ; *veinigi gagathati*, to bite one another. *vei* 1 ; *ni* 4. V. *veihi*.

veitotovigi, to split up a village ; dissension. *vei*.

veituagi, to altercate, strive ; altercation. *vei.*

veitugu(gna), star. M. *vitu* ; Fl. *veitugu.*

veiveri v.t., to fan : *bali veiveri*, a fan. S. *tetere.*

vele v.t., to say to, speak to, address, tell, tell of, speak of, say : *vele huhuru*, to be urgent, instant : *vele peo*, to defend in speech ; *vele puhi*, to teach, to be correct ; *vele daudamu*, to slander ; *vele saropagini*, to sneer at ; *vele tona*, to mock ; *vele vunagi*, to speak in a loud voice ; *vele ngangata*, to challenge, defy.

faveevele v.t., to speak against.

veleagna gerund.

velelalaulu, unity, amity.

vena, crocodile.

vera, courtyard, open space in village. S. *hera* ; L. *fera.*

vere, to wonder, wonder at ; used with *ni* 1.

vetula v.t., to command ; a command, commandment. (*veuvetula*).

vetulagna gerund.

veuvehuhu, to compete, overtake : *rage veuvehuhu*, to run a race.

veuveruga i mata, eyelash. V. *vulusi.*

vevega, to defæcate, to rust ; excrement, rust. S. *he'a* ; V. *vega.*

vi 1, trans. suffix to vb. : *dorovi.* Fl. *vi.*

vi 2, prefix to numeral *tolu* : *vitolu*, third day. Wedau, New Guinea *vi.*

viaviha, to devise.

vidi, to be in labour, of women : labour pains. Fl. *vidi.*

vido v.t., to divide into portions ; a portion, piece, place ; some : *vido i magavu*, an hour (late) ; *vido i mamatho*, respite ; *vido i vinoga*, a season of the year ; *ke toke sina vido mua*, a little more will do ; *ke boi bohe sina vido*, it is not at all heavy ; *gnami vidogna*, to taste of ; *sa vidogna*, a piece of it. Fl. *vido.* (*viovido*).

vidoa, in part.

vidoagna gerund.

vihuki v.t., to pluck fruit, etc., to behead. V. *savi.*

viuvihukiagna gerund.

vihuvunagi, name of a marriage clan. *vunagi.* *posomogo* ; *thonggokama.*

vike(gna) 1, a household, a man's personal following, the people of a place : *mara na vike*, Gentiles (late).

vike 2, to withstand, contend, oppose, resist ; contention. (*vievike*).

vili v.t., to choose. S. *hili* ; Fl. *vili.*

vilihai red shell-money, of ten strings, a fathom long.

vinahi(gna), flesh, lean meat. S. *hinesu* ; V. *venesi* ; Fl. *vinahi.*

vinahuhu(gna), exogamous clan. Fl. *vinavahuhu*, people.

vinaru, to weed a kumara garden.

vinata, to pay money on the death of a chief to avoid being raided : *bali vinata*, a ransom by the giving of money or a life.

vinoga, the time of ripe canarium almonds, the winter, a season : *vinoga koso*, winter ; *vinoga i gegeli*, harvest time, yam digging.

vio(gna), penis. *fio*.

viri 1, to be twisted, tangled, mysterious, wonderful : *ke viri na hehenggu*. I wondered at it ; *viri nago*, to carry coconuts on a pole over the shoulder, in front and behind. S. *hiri* ; Fl. *viri*.

viri 2, English twist tobacco. L. *firi*.

virigi v.t., to wind round, to be overgrown with creepers, to bind in bundle ; a bundle.

viriloga, whirlwind, tempest. *lologa*. V. *viriloha*.

vitatha, to beckon : *athaatha vitatha*, the beckoning crab.

vitili v.t., to flash through, of lightning or gun flash. Fl. *viti*.

vitu, numeral seven. S. *hiu*.
   vavitugna, seventh.
   vitugna, seventh.

viuvihu, the men's chant at a death.

viviloho, to roll up, fold.

voga, a fishing stage, tripod.

vogiriu, to be dislocated, out of joint : *riu*. Fl. *vogi*.

voivoringgi, to creak.

voki(gna), chamber in house, cupboard. Fl. *voki*.

voko, a basket.

vonggu, a wave before it breaks, a swell.

voli v.t., to buy, sell, pay ; price : *na hava kotida nia voliugna*, what will you pay me ? Fl. *voli*. (*voivoli*).

voliagna gerund, to buy, sell, pay ; price.

volo : *hai volo, huia na volo*, to eat to excess.

vonu, to be full ; fulness : *ke hangga vonu*, it is nearly full ; *na vonugna*, its fulness. *hungu* ; S. *honu* ; Fl. *vonu*.

vavonu v.t., to fill.

vavonungi v.t.

vonua adj., full.

vonungi v.t., to fill, be full of.

vonungiagna gerund.

vognu, turtle. S. *honu* ; Fl. *vonu*.

voovogo, to bind as a belt ; a belt, girdle : *piri voovogo*, a belt. S. *ho'o*.

voovogoagna gerund.

vora, to swell ; a bodily swelling. *vorangi* v.t., to puff up, swell out. Fl. *vorahi*, to spread.

voti, to break up.

votu, to go away, go on a canoe journey. Ed., Fl. *votu*.

vothoha, the time of growing yams, November to March, a season.

vovoga, to mediate, interpose, to separate two combatants ; a mediator. Fl. *voga* ; S. *hoa*.

vua, crocodile. S. *huasa* ; Fl. *vua*.

vuavula, whale.

vudi, plantain, banana. Fl. *vudi*.

vuevungge, crumbs, bits of food. Fl. *vuevungge*.

vugei, in the morning, this morning : *ke vuevugei*, in the morning. *vugoi*.

vugoi, to be early afoot in the morning, in the future, time to come : *vugoi valiha*, in the future, time to come ; *kenugua vuovugoi*, to-morrow morning ; *vuovugoi puni*, before daylight ; *na vuovugoigna*, next day. *vugei* ; *vavugo*. S. *hu'o* ; R. *vugo* ; Fl. *vuvugo*.

vuha, to begin, to be, become, appear, to conceive, be born : *vuha hagore*, to bear false witness, take a false oath, to reproach ; used with *i* 3, to denote ' become ', ' be ', ' till ', ' until ' : *nggi e vuhai jufu ke anggai eni*, up till the present time ; *ke eia na bea nggi e vuhai wine*, turned the water into wine ; *na vuhagna*, because of. Fl. *vuha.* (*vaavuha*).

vavuha v.t., to beget, bring forth, produce, make, create.

vavuhagna gerund.

veivuavuha hagoregi, to speak evil of one another.

vuavuhagna gerund., conceiving.

vuhu v.t., to shoot with arrow or gun. V. *tuvu* ; M. *us*, a bow. (*vuuvuhu*).

vui, to swing on a swing, to swing about : *ke vuivui na kolagna*, his liver swings, he is in terror. S. *huihui*.

vuchi 1, to go rapidly, do rapidly : *vuchi ma na onga ke nggovu*, he did it in a flash.

vuchi 2, to branch out, send out branches.

vula(gna) 1, moon, month : *na vulagna*, its month. M. *vula*.

vula 2, to arrive, appear, come out, emerge ; appearance : *vula au*, to go out into ; *vula hadi*, to enter ; *na togulu i vula*, strangers arriving. U. *hula* ; R. *vura*. (*vuavula*).

veivulangigi, to meet at a village, of parties, to encounter.

vulala, steam.

vuli v.t., to wash a person, to pour water on, quench : *vulia na dikatagna*, to appease his wrath. Fl., V. *vuli*. (*vuivuli*).

vulodo, a spark.

vulu(gna), feather, hair. S. *hulu*. *vuvuluga* adj., hairy.

vunagi(gna), chief, a full-grown person, master : *a vunagidia*, their master. Fl. *vunagi* ; M. *vunai*, upper part.

vune(gna), base, bottom, beginning, origin, trunk of tree : *na vunegna*, because of.

vunu(gna), outer skin of canarium almond.

vunugi v.t., to deliver up, hand over to the enemy, sell. Fl. *vunugi*.

vunuha, sacred place where men wait while the sacrifice is being offered. Fl. *vunuha*.

vungao(gna), relations-in-law. S. *hungao* ; Fl. *vungo*.

vungu, to bear fruit, be plentiful ; bunch of almond nuts or bananas ; ears of corn. S. *hungu* ; V. *vungu*. (*vuuvungu*).

vuovutho, to flick.

vuovuthotho(gna), successor, heir : *kena vuovuthothogna*, they succeeded him.

vupa, to go out, of fire.

vuraga, to be in abundance, flourish ; abundance, increase. V. *vuraha*.

vavuraga, to bear abundantly.

vureaja, low lying, flat, of island.

vurehe v.t., to spread out, unfold, be open, free, at liberty. Fl. *vurehi* ; V. *vuresi.*

vavurehe v.t., to free, deliver.

vavureheagna gerund., freeing, to free.

vurehea passive, free : *na tinoni seka ke bosi vurehea,* a slave is not free.

vuru 1, fish scales. Fl. *vuru.*

vuru 2, to scrape, scratch.

vurukusu, to cut or slash off, cut in two.

vurukusuagna gerund.

vuse, scabies.

vusu, to bud, shoot ; a shoot. V. *tuvu* ; Fl. *puputu.*

vuti v.t., to pluck up by the roots. Fl. *vuti.* (*vuivuti*).

vutu, a tree, barringtonia. Fl. *vutu* ; S. *huu.*

vuthea, specific numeral, a million, used of canarium almonds : *na vuthea.* Fl. *vule,* much.

vuthothagini v.t., to reveal to.

vuuvuu onomatop., the mason wasp.

vuvuhu, whitlow.

vuvulu, the leaf of the betel pepper.

vuvuriju, to do earnestly, thoroughly, altogether, none missing.

INDEX

A

a, *na, sa, si na.*
abate, *gnao.*
abhor, *duaduma, siriuhagini.*
abide, *mono, tove.*
abort, *kavuvu.*
about, *kilili, kolili* ; *eu.*
above, *popo.*
absorbed, *soropi.*
abstain, *bati.*
abundance, *salage i thaba, vuraga.*
abundantly, *liuleva.*
abuse, to, *langgu, tongari, vele tona.*
accursed, *kakabakeha.*
accuse, *baro, tahotha, toro.*
across, *baabala.*
active, *sasaa, sasaapiro.*
add, *pisangi, togolo.*
adhere, *thangu.*
adopt, *taenggo.*
adorn, *gnilau.*
adult, *mane gano, pau ni mane, tinoni puhi.*
adultery, *goho, ngelengele.*
afflict, *kaekathe, paapara.*
after, *nggovu, legu.*
afternoon, *kavaligi.*
again, *goi, gua, piliu.*
against, *kene, pungusi.*
agony, *giigidi, kaekathe.*
agreement, *fari hagore, sakai godo, sakai hagore.*
aground, *sara.*
ague, *mathaho.*
aim, *kaekane, keekene.*
air, *manga.*
alive, *havi.*
all, *nggounggovu ; hihovu, udolu.*
allow, *lubati.*

almost, *hangga.*
alone, *gehe, hege.*
already, *gohi.*
also, *gua.*
always, *hahali.*
amiss, *pedo.*
among, *hotagi, ita.*
ancestor, *hutu, kue, kuekue.*
anchor, *piniti.*
and, *ma, kari.*
anger, *ahavagi, dikata, ngaengate.*
ankle-bone, *buibuli i nae.*
annoy, *buebule, faeiei.*
anoint, *tasu.*
another, *sikei, sina.*
answer, *hagore tugu.*
ant, *ane, duki, kogno, sotha, thotho.*
anus, *kato, bili sisi moro.*
any, *sa.*
apart, *sopa, tavoga.*
appear, *tate.*
approach, *jutu.*
areca, *biu, etieti.*
arise, *sokara.*
arm, *lima.*
armlet, *bakiha, hokata, seli.*
armpit, *baibalige.*
around, *kilili, kolili.*
arrive, *jufu, laba, sapa, vula.*
arrow, *kuali, sia.*
as, *vaga.*
ascend, *hadi, kotu, vara.*
ashamed, *maomamo.*
ashes, *parafu, pidaravu, ravu.*
ashore, *sara.*
ask, *huati, kae.*
askance, *leeleve.*
assemble, *haidu, hatha tango, goromagi mai, tatanggutu.*
assent, *hii.*

boast, *gaegahe.*
body, *tono.*
boil, *futu, ngguanggura* ; *puguli.*
bold, *fasiisiri, irupono, kikitiri.*
bone, *huli.*
bonito, *atu.*
booth, *babale, sakapa.*
bore, *aruaru, bilo* ; *buebule.*
border, *nohi.*
borrow, *raii.*
bottle, *duee, cheu.*
bottom, *kea, vune.*
bow n., *bage.*
bow v., *malehenggo, pogo horu, oogo.*
bowl, *duee, lapa, nahu, popo.*
boy, *nggari mane.*
brackish, *hulumaruarua.*
brain, *korongasa.*
branch, *otooto* ; *gaba* ; *base hangana.*
breadfruit, *hego, popone.*
break, *fike, fota, nana, nggotihi, pido, poha, renggohi, tautu, tatohu, tifi.*
breast, *rangga, susuu.*
breath, *aheahe.*
bride, *vaivine taulagi* ; -groom, *mane taulagi.*
bright, *salemage.*
brightness, *silada.*
brimful, *jata, piditao.*
bring, *hati.*
brother, *tahi, toga, vavine* ; -in-law, *iva* ; *vungao.*
bruise, *bakai, boabotha, nggola, mapongga, tula.*
brush, *penutu* ; *hatha, tungge.*
bubble, *buaburara, fuufutu, nggua-nggura.*
bud, *tapurese.*
build, *hati, hothati, ruru, tiitili, tutu, utuhi* ; *kaju.*

bump, *saba.*
bunch, *vungu.*
bundle, *boo, file, vagu.*
bung, *fufulo.*
burden, *hoahotha.*
burn, *juru, poipodilo, pugujuru, siriki* ; *guguvu.*
burst, *poha.*
bury, *kuvuri, nggilu, vakoli.*
bush, *hothoho, jao, legelai* ; *baabagnaga, tutuguru.*
busy, *nggipo, gnabo, ponoi, runggusi, sasaa.*
but, *kari, keana.*
butterfly, *aoalo.*
buttock, *moro.*
buttress, *lali.*
buy, *sabiri, voli.*
by, *ita.*
by and by, *kenugua, kikimua, magugua.*

C

cabbage, *gnahi.*
call, *jathe, kilo, kuakuala.*
calm, *paa horu, sola, soto.*
camp, *piniru.*
canoe, *hinage* ; *biabina, keda, peko, sosoro, tola, tomoko.*
canoe-house, *kiala.*
cape, *giju, sapa.*
careful, *tataji, vavuriju.*
careless, *faefaje, hailasa, lau saba, memenggili, gnagugnege, pono hehe.*
cargo, *luluja.*
carry, *achi, avini, bebere, beebee, bini, galalu, hobi, hotha, hulu, kodo, laolako, ooho, palakue, papa, rosa, sutu.*
carve, *kaju, rarahi, sasari.*
castrate, *thaho.*

cast skin, *ugnu.*
catch, *kau, laku, sakuri.*
caterpillar, *muno.*
cat's cradle, *ra-u.*
caulk, *muki.*
cave, *kato, luma.*
cease, *hui, nggovu, tautu.*
centipede, *liva.*
certain, *kekeha, si na* ; *togokale.*
certainly, *mugua.*
chamber, *voki.*
champion, *duili, mathagai.*
chance, *hai.*
change, *oli, tugu.*
channel, *hunua, jari, sulupu.*
charm, *bei, ruaruva, toe, thako.*
chase, *paji.*
chatter, *kiokido, thavu hagore.*
cheek, *bako.*
cherish, *taenggo.*
chew, *nggunggumu, ngangata.*
chief, *vunagi* ; *nago, tinaulu.*
child, *dathe, nggari, meomeo.*
chin, *ngoengoe.*
choke, *lulugua, vaivaligo, virigi.*
choose, *magnahagi, vahi, vili.*
chop, *miumisu, piopido, toka.*
clam, *tungi.*
clap, *tapo.*
clasp, *pugnoku, thoti.*
claw, *gugu.*
clean, *gnagura, raraha.*
clean, to, *hatha.*
cleanse, *lumi.*
clear, *sanggala* ; *salemage* ; *samo, tobi, tuvati.*
cleave, *pahala, thevurua* ; *panguti.*
cliff, *mije, tietinggele.*
climb, *asikeba, habira, kangguli, saki hage.*
clip, *kokoju, koto, utuutu.*
close, *kabolagini, pono, savu.*
close by, *laubano.*

cloth, *pohe, poko.*
clothe, *huha, oopo.*
cloud, *parako, puni.*
cloudy, *kuukumu, sausavu.*
club, *tila.*
clumsy, *savusolu.*
cockatoo, *guagua.*
cockroach, *muhu.*
coconut, *niu, koilo* ; *kaokagno, kurohu* ; *kokomo, penutu.*
collect, *hathatano.*
cold, *gaula* ; *mathaho.*
comb, *katha.*
come, *kalasu, mai, sapa, vano, vula.*
comfort, *kaso, sula.*
command, *vetula.*
commit, *livusagi, tamathagi.*
companion, *dua, kamane, uduudua.*
company, *boo, hagata.*
compare, *hagore koiliu, juajuka.*
compel, *huhuru.*
complain, *huahungga.*
complete, *kasa, nggovu, pisupa, taudolu, udolu* ; *puku.*
compress, *huru, pamu.*
conceal, *paligi, polohagini, tokuvi.*
conceive, *boebote, vuha.*
couch, *tavuli.*
conduct, *talangi.*
confident, *tongga, thangga.*
confusion, *ruubala.*
consequence, *nggi.*
consent, *hii.*
consume, *gani, pugujuru.*
contrary, *halu tavoga* ; *juloto, puchaoko, veevene* ; *kene.*
continual, *talu, tuutuu teeteve, tuutuu loalova.*
convalescent, *gaota.*
cook, *duee, kuro, ngguanggura, paapara, pugu, siisiri.*
cooked, *mamoha.*

coral, *kuri*.
cord, *atho, gatho, piru*.
cork, *fufulo, pakoto*.
corner, *dou, chogo, kuli*.
corpse, *kiri, thamuta*.
corrupt, *boto, gnarutu, songge*.
costly, *vahothagini*.
cough, *gajika, kajiga, ouou*.
count, *iju*.
covenant, *sakai hagore*.
cover n., *fufulo, mata*.
cover v., *kuikuvi, pungusi, tafu, togahi, tokuvi*.
covet, *nggeunggevuga, mamanggo, poopongo*.
crab, *athaatha vitatha, kakau, kapote, koba, ragomu, tubutha, urio*.
crack, *raraja, singgo* ; *poapoha*.
crackle, *nggaenggarere*.
crafty, *gaea*.
cramp, *reka*.
crane, *kopi*.
crash, *rete, tanggumu*.
crawfish, *ura*.
crawl, *kanggu*.
creeper, *atho, tuva*.
crest, *palala*.
cripple, *kodo*.
crocodile, *vena, vua*.
crook, *gaba, ikonga*.
crooked, *lioliko*.
cross over, *hathavu, pelo, pothoho*.
crouch, *tarago*.
crowd, to, *hunguti, nggungguvi, pisi kilili* ; n. *hagata, tatha*.
crushed, *maruha*.
cry, *giagila, guu, jathe, keke, kuakuala, lovogata, rorojo, sale tangi, tangi*.
cubit, *kado i huli*.
cup, *hinao, seu*.
cupboard, *pao*.

current, *thaithavi*.
curse, to, *fafarangagi*.
cursed, *kakabakeha*.
custom, *puhi*.
cut, *kaju, miumisu, pahe, songgi, talugau, utuutu*.
cut off, *dere, kajari, tarakusu, utuhi*.

D

daily, *leulegu magavu*.
dam, *liutuu*.
damp, *gaula*.
dance, *laulahu, ranggi, sepe*.
danger, *hoholo, thehe haihavi*.
dark, *puni, puni doka, rodopono*.
darkness, *rodopono, rodopuni, romo*.
daughter, *dathe vaivine* ; -in-law, *vungao*.
dawn, *dani raraha, thabota*.
day, *magavu* ; *dani, hinaota*.
deaf, *pui*.
deaf mute, *oleo, mui, pui*.
dearth, *magnahagi*.
death, *thehe*.
debt, *kibo, pora, talu vata*.
decay, *boto, galume*.
deceit, *muamugna, peopenggo*.
deceive, *pilau, muamugnali, vajefe*.
decided, *gagana tautu, lio sikei*.
declare, *tateli, tuturi au*.
decline, *kavaligi, ligi*.
deep, *horuga, maha*.
defæcate, *vevega*.
defence, *hagore peo, sausaku* ; *vatada*.
defraud, *pongo, vajovo*.
delay, *ngara nguungutu, gnaognabo*.
deliver, *tamathagini*.
denude, *kobathagini*.

G *

earnestly, *vuvuriju*.

earth, *tano*, *thepa*.

earthquake, *agnu*.

easy, *maamatha, malumu, tarutata*.

eat, *gani, tamaji, vanga*.

ebb, *ke sapa na kalai* (*karango*), *maolagi*.

edge, *kokoto*.

eel, *kasa, oloi*.

egg, *kidoru*.

elbow, *puloku*.

elder, *kuekue*.

ember, *koukovuru*.

embrace, *pala, thoti*.

empty, *ali* ; *koba, pasa, peso, sanggala*.

enchantment, *toe* ; *mana*.

enclose, *peopeo, pilu*.

encounter, *hara pada, jatavi*.

end, *kokoto, kujuku, ulu* ; *tautu*.

endure, *gathapaku, ni rava*.

enemy, *kana, tatha, thevu i oka*.

enough, *naba, toke*.

entangled, *vahotha, virigi*.

enter, *hage, iru, chiu, sulupu*.

entice, *seuselu*.

entrust, *kabokili, livusagi, tama-thagi*.

envy, *doodoro leeleve*.

equal, *juka, mana, naba*.

erase, *ruja*.

err, *hahi, jefe*.

error, *paluha*.

escape, *gogo, haliu*.

establish, *kaputi*.

estuary, *jae*.

even, *dadali* ; *hitagi, mugua*.

evening, *lavi*.

example, *palabatu*.

exceedingly, *puala*.

excess, *tomaga*.

exchange, *oli, juajuka, palaolihi*.

excited, *mangginggi, tuu*.

exit, *rugu au*.

expect, *pitu, rouronu*.

extinct, *luvu*.

extinguish, *paa*.

extract, *bio, sipa*.

eye, *mata* ; -lash, *veuveruga i mata* ; -lid, *koakota i mata*.

F

face, *mata*.

fade, *kumusi*.

faggot, *punui, tautu i gai*.

fail, *salupa*.

faithful, *kakai*.

faint, *gnanggo, malesua, manggoli, tavangguluva*.

fall, *horu, kutu, rote, sikili*.

fame, *rongoraga*.

family, *tamadathe, tamatahi, vike, vinahuhu*.

famine, *ngengere*.

fan, *veiveri*.

far, *hau*.

fast, to, *godo, papari, sota*.

fat, *oiobili, popotoio* ; *ragova*.

father, *lufa, mama, tama* ; -in-law, *vungao*.

fathom, *hangava*.

fear, *bobolo, matagu, mauni*.

fearless, *irupono, maa*.

feast, *areare, dokulu, hiroku* ; *vakasa magavu*.

feather, *sesehu, vulu*.

feel, *vajangi*.

fellow, *dua, kamane, uduudua*.

fellowship, *haidu, faidu*.

female, *vaivine*.

fence, *peoti, pilu* ; n., *peo*.

few, *gathi, gnagu, taataha, vaiso*.

field, *anggutu, taliao*.

fight, *rihu*.

fill, *huhuri, purusagi, toi, tolojo, vavonu*.

fillet, *fiifiri ulu, tari ulu.*
filter, *binu.*
filthy, *garu, kore.*
fin, *bagi.*
find, *regipada.*
finger, *kaukau i lima.*
finish, *hui, nggovu, tautu.*
fire, *joto* ; -brand, *pinarasa* ;
    -wood, *gathautu.*
firefly, *dodo.*
firm, *kakai, maku, ngasi, totho* ;
    paingoti, thangga.
firmament, *maaloa.*
first, *nago, nago vahui* ; -born,
    kamanago ; -fruits, *thavinago.*
fish, *fei, iga* ; v., *daudau, taotago,*
    thagi, vagoda.
fish-hook, *penggu, tago.*
fishing-net, *bau, gala, jaraha, jau,*
    ria, tena.
fishing-rod, *guema, rofe.*
fitting, *ulaga.*
five, *lima.*
fix, *kaputi.*
flame, *beubethu.*
flash, *vitili.*
flatter, *muamugna, ngoingovi.*
flay, *guliti.*
flee, *gogo, jikehagini.*
flesh, *vinahi.*
flick, *vuovutho, tautamuhi.*
flint, *nadi.*
flock, *boo, ujatha.*
flood, *biringita, obo, rano, soara,*
    thaithavi.
flourish, *jautovu, liuleva.*
flow, *bouboru, sasalala.*
flower, *runggu.*
flutter, *siviole.*
fly, *thango* ; v. *aapolo, thovo.*
foam, *pachangguanggura.*
fog, *kokopono.*
fold, *lopo, viviloho.*

follow, *legu.*
food, *oho, vanga.*
fool, *buebule, meemee.*
foot, *nae.*
forbid, *hogatha, luti* ; *sa, sagoi,*
    tabu.
forehead, *hoho, lange.*
forenoon, *dani.*
forest, *jao.*
forget, *hahilagini, havagini, madoa,*
    toga sani.
forgive, *talu toga, toga sani.*
formerly, *jangigna.*
forsake, *kavelu, koroga, livusa-*
    gini.
fortress, *toa.*
foundation, *foko, kokoto, sosoloho,*
    tiotinoni.
fountain, *futu.*
four, *vati.*
fowl, *kokiroko, manu.*
free, *mamaluha, vurehea* ;   v.,
    lubati.
freely, *leea, liuleva.*
fresh, *mathangani.*
friend, *kula.*
frigate-bird, *belama.*
fringe, *jeujemuru.*
frog, *chagao, kuikuli, kulau, roa.*
from, *ita, ta.*
fruit, *gano, sagaro.*
fruitless, *pagana.*
full, *hungu, mahu, purusagi, tada-*
    kola, vonu.
full-grown, *pote.*
fungus, *puu.*
furtive, *gaea.*

G

gain, *anggo, maliolio, soni tuta.*
garden, *anggutu, lelegai, mathathe,*
    taliao.
garfish, *mathothe.*

gather, *boo, haidu, haohatho, liboro, sikomi*.

gaze, *buta, dorovi*.

generation, *panggusu*.

generous, *dotho, keukemu*.

gentle, *bugoro, ngaengare*.

gently, *kikimua*.

ghost, *tidatho*.

gift, *dotho* ; *liulivu*.

gimlet, *aruaru*.

ginger, *konggu*.

gird, *kabesau*.

girl, *nggari vaivine*.

give, *he, liulivu, lubati*.

glad, *lealeaa, ngiingili, tootonggo*.

glory, *rongoraga, silada*.

glossy, *loso*.

glow, *gatha*.

gnash teeth, *ngiri kei*.

go, *atu, ausapa, hage, halu, kalasu, lilihi, rugu au, sapa, taviti, vano, votu*.

good, *toke*.

graft, *panggu*.

grain, *peda*.

grandchild, *kukua* ; -father, *kue* ; -mother, *kave*.

grasp, *pognoi*.

grass, *buuburu, nggungguru, sesehu*.

grasshopper, *cheche*.

grate, *aaha, miumisu*.

grave, *beku, lodu*.

grey-headed, *ufa*.

graze, *saba*.

great, *hutu, thaba*.

greedy, *oluolu, ririti*.

grief, *kookono*.

grieve, *dikahehe*.

groan, *nggoenggoe*.

grope, *haranggano, tabo*.

ground, *thepa*.

grove, *buugulu, huguru, kongga, rata*.

grow, *biobiroro, bulou, fuufutu, kotu*.

grumble, *nguungunu*.

grunt, *uiumi*.

guess, *hagore kolanga, tuguni*.

guide, *konggulagini, nagovi, tagao, udu*.

guile, *sula*.

gums, *roai*.

gun, *kukuro*.

gush, *bouboru, futu*.

H

Hades, *Tuhilagi*.

hail, *guu, jathegi*.

hair, *sesehu, vulu*.

hammer, *idathe, silikata* ; *tupi, tupipuhi*.

hand, *lima* ; *madotho, toi*.

handful, *agu*.

handiwork, *matha i lima*.

handle v., *pepetei, tabo, tangoli* ; n., *bali tatango*.

hang, *labutao, ligo, pataka, savera, uru*.

hanker, *tutumulio*.

happen, *pada*.

harbour, *hugu*.

hard, *maku, ngasi, ngutu, patu nggama*.

hardly, *hangga*.

harlot, *kikirase*.

harm, *diadikala*.

harp, *kinggulu, kodili*.

harvest, *baore* ; n., *gegeli, liboro*.

haste, *aanga, rage, saininggi, saisami*.

hastily, *daudamu, samingi*.

hat, *kepi*.

hatch, *ofi, poda*.

hate, *kekebihagini, siriu*.

haul, *tuva*.

haze, *lavo.*
hazy, *sausavu.*
he, *manea.*
head, *pau, uulu.*
healed, *mavo.*
hear, *varongo.*
heart, *hehe, kurijelu, kutu.*
heat, *guguvu, rarangi.*
heaven, *i popo, maaloa.*
heavy, *bohe, nggungguvu, tahu.*
heedlessly, *faefaje, ponohehe.*
heel, *doudou i nae.*
henceforth, *valiha.*
herd, *boo, pangga, ujatha.*
here, *eeni, eeri, na.*
hew, *jou.*
hiccough, *sosonota.*
hide, *peopeo, polo, talu polo.*
higgledy-piggledy, *gnagugnege.*
high, *hadi, teve.*
hill, *bobo, pelo, pokusu, suanuro, suasupa.*
hinder, *valiutuu.*
hiss, *suusuu.*
hit, *hogovi, kathe, pada, puipusi, tupi, thabu.*
hold, *gani, saraki, tangoli.*
hole, *bora, kato, lodu.*
hollow, *longgu, pinu* ; v., *joujou, kololo.*
holy, *tabu.*
hoof, *gugu.*
horizon, *piricho.*
hot, *guguvu, igne, paapara.*
house, *tengguru, vako, vathe.*
how, *ivei ke ania.*
how many, *e ngiha.*
howl, *auakuku, saasangara*
hump-backed, *poguru.*
hundred, *hathangatu.*
hundred thousand, *feferi.*
hunger, *rofo.*
hurry, *aanga.*

hurt, *higiti, paapara.*
husband, *tau.*
husk v., *kago* ; n., *penutu.*
hut, *aava, babale, sakapa.*
hypocrite, *gaegahe, tango poopolo.*

I

I, *inau, nau, u.*
idiot, *aiani.*
idle, *toali.*
idly, *gnaegnave.*
if, *da, nggi.*
ignorant, *hahilagini, paipaligi.*
ill, *vahagi.*
image, *donga, ngunguju.*
immature, *koso.*
immorality, *koakoa, gnognoro.*
impale, *soka, suki.*
importune, *kekelagini, kilo hahali, kilo meemee.*
in, *i, kora, sungga, tagna.*
incessantly, *joijongi.*
incline, *ligi, pogo.*
increase, *jautovu, vuraga.*
indeed, *hitagi, ri, vamua.*
indigo, *pau.*
infant, *meomeo.*
infirm, *lae.*
inherit, *tamaga, vuovuthotho.*
inlay, *sesere.*
insecure, *magohu, nere.*
inside, *kora, i kora, i sungga.*
insipid, *beabeaga.*
instrument, *bali.*
intervene, *hogatha.*
intercept, *sariutu.*
intestines, *kutu kokoilo, kutu loolopo.*
into, *i, kori.*
iron, *jagimaha, valau.*
ironwood, *gugula, tubi.*
irritate, *parangaha.*

island, *moumolu.*

itch, *ngganggaru, mumuka, sirapa.*

J

jaw, *ngoengoe.*

jealous, *tahotha lio.*

jest, *leuleu, theuthehu.*

jew's harp, *mike.*

join, *hathatano, panggu, totho.*

joint, *kado, tuturu.*

joke *leuleu.*

joyful, *lealea, ngiingili.*

judge, *fate, vahi.*

juice, *bea, kotho.*

jump, *peperiki, songgala* ; *gatha-umi.*

K

keep, *palikuti.*

kernel, *tafi.*

kick, *kio.*

kill, *thabu, thamuta, vathehe.*

kind, *faafata, thanggi.*

kindle, *juru, tafuni, vagatha.*

kingdom, *huguta.*

kinsfolk, *kamane.*

kiss, *hiihigini, soisopi.*

kite, *dala.*

knee, *tuturu.*

kneel, *torongagi tuturu.*

knife, *gau, papahe.*

knock, *kiikidi.*

knot, *tarariju, varipuku.*

know, *ado, githatha, thaothadoga.*

L

labour (childbirth), *ngutu, vidi.*

lack, *hai pagana.*

ladder, *rangana.*

lady, *auboro.*

lake, *kolo.*

lame, *saveo, thogu.*

lament, *tangihi.*

lamp, *juta, lui.*

land, *meleha, thepa, vanua* ; v., *tatapa (teteri) i thonga.*

language, *hagore.*

large, *babi, hutu* ; *gothapa.*

last, to be, *kujukui, legu vahui.*

laugh, *kia.*

launch, *sobo, tuva.*

layer, *faafata.*

lazy, *toali.*

lead, *batu, konggulagini, nagovi, talangi, udu.*

leaf, *eloelo.*

leak, *lulu.*

lean, *kavaligi, suato, tuavarava, ulu.*

leave, *boo, livusagini, tavalili.*

leg, *nae.*

lend, *juka.*

lest, *gua e, minggoi.*

let down, *hui, tororo, uli.*

lever, *taitangi.*

lick, *gnagnapi.*

lie (falsehood), *muamugnali, pia-pilau.*

lie down, *koli.*

lift, *abe hadi, hulu.*

light n., *hinara, juta, laema, lui, marara* ; v., *tafuni, totha.*

light (not heavy), *maamatha, ngaengare.*

lighten, *raraha, silada, valaema.*

lightning, *onga.*

like, *ke vagagna, naba, mana, vaga.*

likeness, *sinathagi.*

lime, *keru.*

limp, *suasuato.*

lintel, *kongga baabara.*

lip, *heuhemu, poapoha i livo, sinanggi.*

listen, *varongo*.
little, *iso, kiki, kikiri*.
live, *havi, mono*.
liver, *ate, kola*.
lizard, *garo, ngo, vava*.
load, *lujagini*.
loafer, *mane iuiu*.
loathe, *duaduma*.
lobster, *luukama*.
log, *tabolo*.
loins, *hotagi, mativi*.
long, *teve*.
loiter, *gnaognabo, ngaranguungutu, poru*.
look, *doodoro, ero, liohi, olaola*.
loose, *unuhi, vamoomogo*.
lop off, *dere, kapi*.
lost, *luvu, pululu*.
loud, *barahaha, lovogata, manggi-nggi, ngangara, urungu*.
louse, *gutu, pouporu*.
love, *dotho*.
lump, *puku*.
lung, *loulogu*.
lust, *maamagna*.

M

maggot, *ulo*.
maiden, *kupi, kaekavelato*.
maimed, *kodo*.
make, *birehi, jari, kaju, sari*.
male, *mane*.
malice, *majora*.
man, *mane, tinoni*.
mangrove, *lelegia*.
many, *komi, pona, sethe, suku*; how many, *engiha*.
mark, *aro, iini*; *tunu*.
market, *bahu, sabiri*.
marry, *taulagi*.
mash, *kiukisu, nahu*.
mat, *matha*.

mean, *kanggiri, nggumao*.
measure, *naba*; n., *gailiga, hangava, kado i huli, kakamo, lopo guema, matha i sono, posilego, tao hathavu, thevu lima*.
meddle, *runggusi pedo*.
meditate, *vinata, vovoga*.
meditate, *nggunggumi*.
meet, *haidu, hara pada, jatavi, saba, soni haidu, veipadagi, veivulangigi*.
melt, *lulu*.
member, *baebase*.
memorial, *tutuana*.
mend, *gaura, jari, ponoti*.
merely, *lee, vamua*.
midday, *hinaota*.
middle, *hotagi*.
midway, *sasara*.
might, *mathagai*.
million, *vuthea*.
mind, *hehe, lio*.
miserable, *koki, raorarovi*.
miss, *haliu*.
mist, *dara, kovesa, lavo*.
mistake, *hahi, gaagana pedo*.
mix, *horujotha, joajotha, ngigno, tamaji*.
mock, *leuleu, theuthehu*.
molest, *kanalagini*.
money, *muomuno, paki, rade, rongo, turabuto, vilihai*.
moon, month, *vula*.
moor, *baorage*.
more, *gua, liu, vano*.
morning, *dani, vuevugei, vuovugoi*.
mosquito, *gnamu*.
moss, *lumusa*.
moth, *aoalo*.
mother, *ido, tina*; -in-law, *vungao*.
mouldy, *nggaru*.

P

paddle, *gagao, guihage, kodoko, saka* ; n., *bakala, jemi.*
pair, *loga.*
panpipes, *ifu.*
pant, *paapanga.*
parable, *hagore koiliu, hagore naba.*
paralytic, *kalabae.*
parcel, *vauvagu.*
parrot, *kiekigne, siviri.*
part, *thevu* ; v., *lebi.*
partake, *faifari.*
pass, *au sumari, hathavu, thovo haliu.*
passage, *hunua, jari, sulupu.*
patch, *gaura, poopono.*
patient, *gathapaku.*
path, *hangana, hathautu.*
pay, *taba.*
pawpaw, *kibo.*
peace, *nanasa, soleana.*
peer, *olaola.*
peg, *konggoro.*
pelt, *piri.*
penis, *gnao, fio, vio.*
penetrate, *suusulupu.*
people, *mara, mavitu, vike.*
perceive, *fagila, rongovi, vajangi.*
perform, *tango.*
perhaps, *bule, gua ri, kanabule.*
perish, *luvu, uri.*
perplexed, *horu haihadi, jalakulu.*
persecute, *kanalagini, papaji.*
persist, *gnabo.*
persistently, *joijongi, tapoto.*
person, *hanu.*
persuade, *suasula, vele huhuru.*
phosphorescent, *rura, tora.*
piece, *pupuruma, vido.*
pierce, *aru, jai, suba, suki.*
pig, *botho.*

pigeon, *baubahulu, bora, kavuku, kuukuu.*
pilfer, *sikodofu, sikopo, vanga kovotho.*
pillow, *ulunga.*
pinch, *kignibi.*
pineapple, *poro.*
pipe, *pipiala.*
pipes, *kuleru, lobere, tuutu* ; play pipes, *ifu.*
pity, *rarovi.*
place, *matha, meleha, vido* ; v. *sobo, talu.*
plague, *kaekathe, leelehe.*
plain, *nata.*
plait, *pijiri, tihigi, toilo, vao.*
plane, *sasigi.*
planet, *gama.*
plank, *pava.*
plant, *jou.*
play, *laulahu, sogo.*
pleased, *maliolio.*
plot, *kuukunu, majora.*
pluck, *biniuki, huri, saka, tagi, vihuki, vuti.*
point, *fiofigno, giju, livo, nuguvotu, sapa.*
point v., *kaekane, keekene, tuhu.*
poison (fish), *hahaga, tuva* ; *maomao.*
poke, *choku.*
pool, *kilionggu, kolo, tiro.*
polished, *dadali, salu.*
poor, *kuma.*
porpoise, *kirio* ; -tooth, *rade.*
portion, *vido.*
possess, *puku, tono.*
possession (demoniacal), *tarongi.*
possible, *tango malaga, tango mana.*
pour, *rote, tilima, toi, vuli.*
powdery, *uvu.*
power, *mana, thaba* ; *heta, nuilagi, sasaalangagi.*

pray, *tarai.*
preach, *titiono.*
prepare, *kaliti, vauvanggu.*
presently, *kenugua, kikimua, magu, magugua.*
press, *huru, puingi.*
prevent, *hogatha, valiutuu.*
profane, *sapu, sido, valisavu.*
prohibition, *sa, sosoka, tabu.*
project, *nago maliu.*
promise, *talu hagore, talu vata.*
property, *tono.*
prosper, *jautovu.*
prostrate, *rago.*
provoke, *geigesi.*
pull, *tuva, thagi.*
pus, *thabutu. thoto.*
push, *hujuu, tuva.*
put, *livu, talu.*
put on, *huha, oopo, sutu, vahage.*
putty-nut, *tita.*

Q

quench, *paa, vuli.*
question, *huati.*
quicksand, *papauro.*
quiet, *bugoro, soto, tongga.*

R

rafter, *gaho.*
rage, *ngaengate.*
rail, *ngara.*
rain, *uha.*
rainbow, *pipiutu.*
ram, *kaakata.*
rapid, *vuchi.*
rashly, *daudamu.*
rat, *kuhi* ; -trap, *tengedeu.*
rattan cane, *gue.*
raw, *deedee.*
reach, *giagila, jufu, laba, torongagi, vula.*

read, *ijumi.*
ready, *ririana.*
real, *puku.*
rebound, *pidi.*
rebuke, *baro, hira, huari, ore, tongari.*
receive, *hati.*
red, *mela, sisi.*
reed, *seo.*
reef, *hagalu, kalai, karango, nuguvotu.*
reel, *kutumaedu.*
refrain, *bati.*
refuse v., *boitagini, hamutagi, hove, huhugu.*
refuse n., *boku, saosagoma.*
reject, *sani.*
rejoice, *tonggotonggo.*
relatives, *kamane, vike.*
release, *lubati.*
remove, *ali, riu, sulaki.*
renew, *baere.*
repay, *tugu kibo.*
repent, *tugu hehe.*
report, *roorongo, titiono.*
resound, *duulali.*
rest, *mamatho, suato* ; *tavoga.*
respect, *jiejike, maimanihihi.*
retire, *sua.*
return, *tabiru.*
revolve, *kavelu, totopiti.*
reward, *taba.*
ribs, *gaogaro.*
ridge, *kokopa, palala.*
ridgepole, *bete.*
right, *jino, kakai.*
ripe, *gano, giri, mada, muji.*
rise, *bugae, hadi, sokara* ; *hungu.*
river, *bea hutu.*
roar, *gaogarohu, tanggumu.*
roast, *siri.*
rock, *gahira* ; v. *eoeto, gaigali.*
rod, *kuokuo i gai, supa.*

roll, *bokihi, gathomi.*
roof, *poguru* ; *have.*
root, *oga* ; v. *hume.*
rope, *piru, oba.*
rot, *boto, furoma, sebi.*
rough, *gneognebo, poipokite, savusolu.*
round, *dodolu, hiliga, kilili, taligu.*
rub, *aaha, gothahi, ngaangaja, gnujuri, ruja, ujuri.*
rudder, *tagao.*
rump, *kea.*
run, *rage.*
rush, *subulo.*
rust, *vevega.*

S

sacrifice, *havugagi.*
sad, *dika hehe, kumeemere.*
sago palm, *ato* ; -leaf, *busi, sasaka.*
salt, *tahi.*
sanctuary, *biibitiana, padagi, vunuha.*
sand, *nahiga.*
sap, *soisoi.*
satisfied, *mahu, tovu.*
save, *vahavi, vaura.*
say, *ahoru, ani, e a, gagua, hagore, vele.*
scales, *vuru.*
scallop shell, *havulu, vago.*
scalp, *pahala.*
scar, *boabotha, tula.*
scatter, *avusagini, oha, rabo, rosavi, soparaka.*
score n., *tutugu.*
scrape, *gothahi, kakari.*
scratch, *ngganggaru.*
screw, *piruki.*
scrotum, *bogo.*
sea, *hagalu, horara, maha, tahi.*
search, *hiro, kaekale.*

season, *vinoga, vula.*
secretly, *polo, talapolo.*
see, *regi, rei.*
seed, *katura.*
seize, *saraki, thoti.*
self, *gehe.*
sell, *voli, vunugi.*
separate, *lebi.*
set, *sobo, vatada, vatotho.*
seven, *vitu.*
sever, *kapi, utuhi.*
sew, *pama, susuki.*
shade, *peopeo, unga* ; v. *tafungi.*
shadow, *ungaunga.*
shallow, *kalai, tada.*
shake, *aiariri, auagnu, biubiru, gaigali, kaikahi, kaukagnu, kavuhi, gnaognato, gnovo, tautamuhi.*
shame, *maomamo.*
share, *faifari.*
shark, *ele.*
sharp, *fiofigno, vaavanga.*
sharpen, *aaha.*
shave, *feilange, goigori, koto, puipuli.*
she, *iia.*
sheathe, *sulupagini.*
shed, *babale, binara* ; v. *salala, tave.*
shell, *bisako, kokomo.*
shelter, *peopeo, rarago.*
shield, *reoreo.*
shine, *hinara, rangi, raraha, silada.*
ship, *jagimaha, nguanguao, vaka.*
shiver, *aiariri.*
shoot, *vuhu, vusu.*
shore, *lau, paritina.*
short, *kudo.*
shoulder, *alo, thego.*
shout, *hihinggi, totovagi, veavela.*
show, *tatele, tuturi.*
shy, *giagina, maomamo.*

stink, *galofa* ; *sibi*.

stir, *geigesi, kaukalu, ngigno, gneognebo*.

stone, *gahira, seosedo*.

store, *hogoni, kaekafe, koko, sela*.

storm, *kaja, koburu, magavu*.

story, *poto, titiono*.

straight, *jino, sodu*.

strain, *binu, kuna, petekuna*.

stranger, *binaboli, hai tinoni*; *rau*.

stray, *jefe, tuotulo*.

stretch, *gaba, gotohi, tuhu, vatara*.

strike, *palaku, pusi, sopu, taitagi, tautamuhi, thabu*.

string, *atho, gatho*.

strip, *kapi, kuikurigi, sasigi*.

stroke, *tasu*.

stumble, *pejuragi*.

strength, *heta*.

stutter, *pepepe, sobu*.

subside, *gnao, maolagi, pulungagi*.

successively, *sogo*.

suck, *susuu*.

suffer, *giigidi, paapara, rava*.

sugar-cane, *ehu*.

sulk, *fauchu, kilahi*.

summon, *hulagini*.

sun, *aho, vaaho*.

sure, *togokale*.

surf, *gnoro*.

surround, *jaura, pilu*.

swallow, *sono*.

swamp n., *ooro*.

sweat, *fuufutu, susunggula*.

sweet, *mami, mugna*.

swell, *vora*.

swim, *otho*.

swing, *athevotho, siuli, vaivui*.

sword, *isi*.

T

tail, *iuigu*.

take, *hati, hobi, sikomi, tangoli*.

take down, *hui*.

taste, *gnami, gnapi, gnou*.

tattoo, *fofohu, isile*.

teach, *tinarai*.

tear n., *kotho (kothobu) i mata*.

tear v., *nana, saasangavi, sanggi, sesu*.

tell, *vele, tateli, tuturi*.

ten, *hangavulu, salage* ; *aba, boka, pangga, piku, tatha, varipuku*.

that, *ari, eri, iangeri, ianggeri, ngeni*.

thatch, *ato, gailiga*.

the, *na, sa, gna* ; pl., *ara, koi, komi, mara*.

then, *nggi*.

there, *ngengeni*.

thereby, *nia*.

they, *iira, imaraira*.

thick, *tuta*.

thigh, *boke, gogoto*.

thin, *baho, fiifidi, manivi, mativi*.

thing, *bali, fata, hanu*.

think, *gaagana, toga*.

thirst, *langasa*.

this, *ani, eeni, na*.

thorn, *karu, kujikaru, vahingoto*.

those, *irangeni*.

thousand, *toga* ; *mola* ; *feferi*.

three, *tolu*.

throat, *laalaka, lua, soosono*.

throb, *mavini, ngungiti, tuutu*.

throng, *hunguti, nggungguvi, pisi kilili*.

throw, *piri, soni*.

thunder, *kukuro, nggumu, rete*.

thus, *anggai, gaonggai*.

tide, *jata, obo* ; *nggeo, variapo* ; *gogovi*.

times, *horu*.

tired, *babao, gnanggc, paapanga, toa*.

to, *regi, tagna, thae, vani*.

tobacco, *lekona, ngerepe, viri.*
to-day, *kenugua, nggeni.*
toe, *kaukau i nae.*
together, *haidu, sakai.*
to-morrow, *vuevugei, vugoi.*
tongs, *ignavi.*
tongue, *thapi.*
too, *gua.*
tooth, *kei, rade.*
top, *palala, piricho, popo, ulu ; taka.*
toucan, *kongo.*
touch, *hinggili, pepetei, tabo, totha, tungge.*
tow v., *oriori, piti konggu.*
tow n., *sama.*
trample, *butuli, tapali.*
tree, *gai.*
trifle, *pipiringgo.*
tripod, *voga.*
trouble, *gügidi, jalakulu, kaekathe, kukigni, para.*
true, *tutuni, utuni.*
trust, *ravita atu, tuavarava.*
try, *auau, pili.*
tumult, *mangginggi, ruubala.*
turn, *beubekuku, ero, gathotho, kavelu, lioliko, panggehi, pingge, pilungi, riu, sualilo.*
turtle, *vognu ; ngapo.*
tusk, *kome.*
twilight, *haludotha.*
twin, *baso.*
twist, *gathotho, gathomi, piruki, toilo.*
twisted, *viri.*
two, *rua, ro.*

U

ulcer, *hibu, kiokilo, tilo, tubi.*
umbrella, *ngehe.*
under, *sara.*
undo, *biniuki, hurupe, uunuhi.*

uneven, *kabauli.*
until, *inggai, tovongai.*
up, *hadi.*
uproot, *huriloka, kukubo, vuti.*
unripe, *deedee, kobusa, koso.*
urine, *mimi.*
utterly, *pisupaa.*

V

vain, *hai, pagana.*
vagina, *kethe.*
valley, *longgu.*
vein, *ula.*
very, *puala, rae, vaho.*
vessel, *kadolulu, nahu, ruavatu, tabili, tahi.*
village, *meleha, ruru.*
violate, *hili, sido, valisavu.*
violent, *reokejo.*
vision, *salingau.*
visit, *sigo, siromi.*
vomit, *lua, lulu.*
vow, *godo, papari.*

W

wag, *biubiru, eoeto, ligimero, nggetu.*
wages, *taba.*
wail, *rorojo, tangi.*
wait, *pitu.*
walk, *aoaso, taviti, teteri, udu.*
wall, *baabara, hidi, peo, tiitili.*
wallow, *loaloga.*
wander, *jeejefe.*
want, *hangga, magnahagini.*
war, *oka.*
warm, *kiakidapu, mangiru, mimiraha, rarange.*
warn, *vavotu.*
wash, *dadaha, havuli, chapo, lumi, ruja, selima, siusiu, tihi.*
wasp, *magnivo.*
waste, *hainggoinggoi, rahe.*

watch, *doodoro, fagila, kaekale, kavena.*

water, *bea* ; v. *vakouri.*

watercourse, *jari* ; -fall, *pota-jimei* ; -spout, *lologa.*

wave n., *gogovi, maragata, gnoro, vonggu* ; *athevotho, nggetu, tautamuhi.*

way, *hangana, hathautu.*

we, *igami, igita.*

weak, *lae, gnanggo, tavangguluva.*

weapons, *tinabe.*

weary, *manggoli, mause, ngae, selebange.*

weather-bound, *boro.*

wedge, *boongi.*

weed v., *tanggi.*

well n., *lodu i bea, seu.*

wet, *gnubu, tobolo.*

whale, *vuavula.*

what, *hava.*

when, *i ngiha* ; *ngihagi* ; *tovongai.*

where, *ivei.*

whirlpool, *biubiru* ; -wind, *viriloga.*

whisper, *ngunguu, vaavaha.*

whistle, *guigui.*

white, *pura.*

whittle, *kafa.*

who, *ahai.*

whole, *hihovu, nggounggovu, langgo, udolu.*

wide, *aba, gothapa, tavotha.*

widow, widower, *boko, thehe sasani.*

wife, *tau.*

wild, *asi.*

wilderness, *lilama, nggou.*

wind n., *ara, guri, kavali, koburu, sapa jae, sokara lau.*

wind v., *fiifiri, gathotho, toilo.*

wing, *alo, lima.*

wink, *aroga, matakuni, thabuhagi.*

wipe, *gujuri, havula, nigotha.*

wise, *tinathagi, thaothadoga.*

with, *dua, ta* ; *nia, niagna.*

wither, *goee, gnago, rango, rapobete.*

woman, *vaivine.*

womb, *kutu.*

wonder, *thare, vere* ; n. *regithehe.*

word, *hagore.*

work, *anggutu, tango.*

world, *maramagna.*

worm, *huguti, keju, odu, ulo.*

worm-eaten, *kololo.*

worthy, *naba, ulaga.*

wound, *ngeso.*

wrap, *huha, mono, pisi, sasaba.*

wrestle, *vaivaligo.*

wring, *poji.*

wrinkle, *nggoenggothe.*

wrong, *dika, hahi.*

Y

yam, *uvi.*

yard, *laalaba.*

yawn, *maomaova.*

yaws, *lualuka.*

year, *vinoga.*

yellow, *angoango, ngongone.*

yes, *hii.*

yesterday, *ignotha* ; day before —, *valiha.*

yet, *mua.*

yoke, *gali ooho, juka.*

you, *igamu, igoe, o* ; *nige, mara, tolu mara.*

youth, *luvaolu* ; *nggari.*

Other Titles from Hippocrene Books . . .

Pilipino titles of interest from Hippocrene:

PILIPINO-ENGLISH/ENGLISH-PILIPINO DICTIONARY AND PHRASEBOOK
120 pages • 3 ¾ x 7 • 0-7818-0451-5 • W • $11.95pb • (295)

PILIPINO-ENGLISH/ENGLISH-PILIPINO CONCISE DICTIONARY
389 pages • 4 x 6 • 5,000 entries • 0-87052-491-7 • W • $8.95pb • (393)

TAGALOG-ENGLISH/ENGLISH-TAGALOG (PILIPINO) DICTIONARY
500 pages • 5 x 8 • 10,000 entries • 0-7818-0683-6 • NA • $29.95hc • (745)

TAGALOG-ENGLISH/ENGLISH-TAGALOG STANDARD DICTIONARY
300 pages • 6 x 9 • 20,600 entries • 0-7818-0657-7 • W • $14.95 • (714)

Other titles of Interest:

Dictionaries

CAMBODIAN-ENGLISH/ENGLISH-CAMBODIAN STANDARD DICTIONARY
355 pp • 5 ½ x 8 ¼ • 15,000 entries • 0-87052-818-1 • NA • $8.95pb • (451)

CHINESE HANDY DICTIONARY
120 pp • 5 x 7 ¾ • 0-87052-050-4 • USA • $8.95pb • (347)

CLASSIFIED AND ILLUSTRATED CHINESE-ENGLISH DICTIONARY, Revised
897 pp • 5 ¼ x 7 ½ • 35,000 entries • 2,000 illust • 0-87052-714-2 • NA • $19.95hc • (27)

ENGLISH-PINYIN DICTIONARY
500 pp • 4 x 6 • 10,000 entries • 0-7818-0427-2 • $19.95pb • USA • (509)

JAPANESE-ENGLISH/ENGLISH-JAPANESE CONCISE DICTIONARY, Romanized
235 pp • 4 x 6 • 8,000 entries • 0-7818-0162-1 • W • $11.95pb • (474)

JAPANESE HANDY DICTIONARY
120 pp • 5 x 7 ¾ • 0-87052-962-5 • $8.95pb • NA • (466)

KOREAN-ENGLISH/ENGLISH-KOREAN PRACTICAL DICTIONARY
365 pp • 4 x 7¼ • 8,500 entries • 0-87052-092-X • Asia and NA • $14.95pb • (399)

KOREAN HANDY DICTIONARY
186 pp • 5 x 7 ¾ • 0-7818-0082-X • W • $8.95pb • (438)

THAI HANDY DICTIONARY
120 pp • 5 x 7 ¾ • 0-87052-963-3 • USA • $8.95pb • (468)

VIETNAMESE-ENGLISH/ENGLISH-VIETNAMESE STANDARD DICTIONARY
501 pp • 5 ½ x 7½ • 12,000 entries • 0-87052-924-2 • W • $19.95pb • (529)

Tutorial

CANTONESE BASIC COURSE
416 pp • 5 ½ x 8 ½ • 0-7818-0289-X • W • $19.95pb • (117)

BEGINNER'S CHINESE
150 pp • 5 ½ x 8 • 0-7818-0566-X • $14.95pb • W • (690)

MASTERING JAPANESE
368 pp • 5 ½ x 8 ½ • 0-87052-923-4 • USA • $14.95pb • (523)
2 Cassettes: • 0-87052-983-8 USA • $12.95 • (524)

BEGINNER'S JAPANESE
200 pp • 5 ½ x 8 ½ • 0-7818-0234-2 • W • $11.95pb • (53)

LAO BASIC COURSE
350 pp • 5 ½ x 8¼ • 0-7818-0410-8 • W • $19.95pb • (470)

BEGINNER'S VIETNAMESE
517 pp • 7 x 10 • 30 lessons • 0-7818-0411-6 • $19.95pb • W • (253)

Cookbooks

THE JOY OF CHINESE COOKING
Doreen Yen Hung Feng
    Includes over two hundred kitchen-tested recipes, detailed illustrations and a thorough index.
226 pp • 5 ½ x 7 ½ • 0-7818-0097-8 • $8.95pb • (288)

History

KOREA: THE FIRST WAR WE LOST, REVISED EDITION
Bevin Alexander
    This bestselling account of the Korean War has now been updated with two additional chapters.
    "Well researched and readable."   *—The New York Times*
    "This is arguably the most reliable and fully-realized one volume history of the Korean War since David Rees' *Korea*."
    —Publisher's Weekly

"Bevin Alexander does a superb job . . .this respectable and fast-moving study is the first to be written by a professional army historian."
—*Library Journal*

Bevin Alexander is a noted journalist who was a combat historian during the Korean War, commander of the 5th Historical Detachment and author of numerous battle studies for the U.S. Army. He resides in Bremo Bluff, Virginia.

580 pp • 13 maps, index • 6 x 9 • 0-7818-0577-5 • W • $19.95pb

DICTIONARY & PHRASEBOOK SERIES

AUSTRALIAN DICTIONARY AND PHRASEBOOK
Helen Jonsen

Displaying the diversity of English, this book provides terms connected with specific situations such as driving, size conversion charts, travel options, and sightseeing trips are just a few of the many topics provided.

131 pp • 4 3 ¾ x 7 • 1,500 entries • 0-7818-0539-2 • W • $11.95pb • (626)

BASQUE-ENGLISH / ENGLISH-BASQUE DICTIONARY AND PHRASEBOOK

240 pages • 3 ¾ x 7 • 1,500 entries • 0-7818-0622-4 • W • $11.95pb • (751)

BOSNIAN-ENGLISH/ENGLISH-BOSNIAN DICTIONARY AND PHRASEBOOK

175 pp • 3 ¾ x 7 • 1,500 entries • 0-7818-0596-1 • W • $11.95pb • (691)

BRETON-ENGLISH/ENGLISH-BRETON DICTIONARY AND PHRASEBOOK

131 pp • 3 ¾ x 7 • 1,500 entries • 0-7818-0540-6 • W • $11.95pb • (627)

BRITISH-AMERICAN/AMERICAN-BRITISH DICTIONARY AND PHRASEBOOK
160 pp • 3 ¾ x 7 • 1,400 entries • 0-7818-0450-7 • W • $11.95pb • (247)

CHECHEN-ENGLISH/ENGLISH-CHECHEN DICTIONARY AND PHRASEBOOK
160 pp • 3 ¾ x 7 • 1,400 entries • 0-7818-0446-9 • NA • $11.95pb • (183)

GEORGIAN-ENGLISH/ENGLISH-GEORGIAN DICTIONARY AND PHRASEBOOK
150 pp • 3 ¾ x 7 • 1,300 entries • 0-7818-0542-2 • W • $11.95pb • (630)

GREEK-ENGLISH/ENGLISH-GREEK DICTIONARY AND PHRASEBOOK
175 pages # 3 ¾ x 7 # 1,500 entries # 0-7818-0635-6 # W # $11.95pb # (715)

IRISH-ENGLISH/ENGLISH-IRISH DICTIONARY AND PHRASEBOOK
160 pp • 3 ¾ x 7 • 1,400 entries/phrases • 0-87052-110-1 NA • $7.95pb • (385)

LINGALA-ENGLISH/ENGLISH-LINGALA DICTIONARY AND PHRASEBOOK
120 pp • 3 ¾ x 7 • 0-7818-0456-6 • W • $11.95pb • (296)

MALTESE-ENGLISH/ENGLISH-MALTESE DICTIONARY AND PHRASEBOOK
175 pp 3 ¾ x 7 • 1,500 entries • 0-7818-0565-1 • W • $11.95pb • (697)

POLISH DICTIONARY AND PHRASEBOOK
252 pp • 5 ½ x 8 ½ • 0-7818-0134-6 • W • $11.95pb • (192)
Cassettes—Vol I: 0-7818-0340-3 • W • $12.95 • (492)
Vol II: 0-7818-0384-5 • W • $12.95 • (486)

RUSSIAN DICTIONARY AND PHRASEBOOK, Revised

256pp • 5 ½ x 8 ½ • 3,000 entries • 0-7818-0190-7 • W • $9.95pb • (597)

UKRAINIAN DICTIONARY AND PHRASEBOOK

205pp • 5 ½ x 8 ½ • 3,000 entries • 0-7818-0188-5 • w • $11.95pb • (28)

All prices are subject to change. To order Hippocrene Books, contact your local bookstore, call (718) 454-2366, or write to: Hippocrene Books, 171 Madison Ave. New York, NY 10016. Please enclose check or money order adding $5.00 shipping (UPS) for the first book and $.50 for each additional title.